Look, It's Books!

Look, It's Books!

Marketing Your Library with Displays and Promotions

Gayle Skaggs

McFarland & Company, Inc., Publishers

Jefferson, North Carolina, and London

LIBRARY OF CONGRESS CATALOGUING-IN-PUBLICATION DATA

Skaggs, Gayle, 1952–
Look, it's books! marketing your library with displays and promotions / Gayle Skaggs.
p.   cm.
Includes index.

ISBN 13: 978-0-7864-3132-8
softcover : 50# alkaline paper ∞

1. School libraries—United States—Marketing.   2. Bulletin boards
in libraries—United States.   3.   Library exhibits—United States.
4. Reading promotion—United States.   I. Title.
Z675.S3S59725   2008   021.7—dc22   2007049517

British Library cataloguing data are available

Cover photograph ©2007 Shutterstock

Manufactured in the United States of America

*McFarland & Company, Inc., Publishers
Box 611, Jefferson, North Carolina 28640
www.mcfarlandpub.com*

To my husband,
who is my best friend,
and to two wonderful friends,
Pat Hoefener and Joyce Scrivner.
They have both loved me and encouraged me
through a difficult time in my life
and I am so grateful for their friendship.

Table of Contents

Preface

Do you secretly dread the thought of a new school year because you will have to put up a new bulletin board, new book displays, and plan those same old library skills lessons? This book is just what you need!

The book is divided into two parts. The first part is designed to offer some practical ideas to market your library services and to help make the school year an awesome one for you and your patrons. The second half is made up of suggested themes for decorating your space plus ideas to promote reading programs.

Introduction

Do you remember the excitement you felt when you first learned to read? What power you possessed! You were suddenly able to make some sense out of the jumble of letters all around you. For many of us that day occurred years ago, but our love for reading has become a life-long passion. What other skill have you learned that you use more than reading?

A good reader doesn't just suddenly appear. The only way to improve one's reading skill is to read and then read some more. Our job as educators is to encourage and motivate the child to read more and thereby improve his or her skill through lots of practice. This book is designed to help the busy elementary or middle school librarian or classroom teacher with suggested ways to promote reading and the library through skills lessons and creative display ideas.

Your library or classroom is in a sense a business. You are selling an education and the enjoyment of reading. Any other business in today's world must include advertising in its business plans. The same is true for the librarian or classroom teacher. The trick is to do this advertising without spending a fortune or using up all of your even more valuable time.

So ... this book may be just what you need. Included are suggestions for displays to promote reading, lessons to teach the Dewey Decimal System, other suggested curriculum helps, general ideas to promote the use of the library and some themes for reading programs. Best of all, these things can be done on a shoestring budget.

With limited funds that must be spread among books, software, equipment, etc., there's often little left for promotion of the program. The novelty soon wears off and then what do you do? What is needed for the long haul is a fantastic, fast idea that will grab the children's interest, is easy to put together, and costs next to nothing.

Use the ideas as they are presented or transform them into just what your school needs. The best thing is that by personalizing the theme to fit your school, you will create a masterpiece. Just say to yourself, "I can do this," and your students will say, "This is awesome!"

Part I

Practical Ideas for Marketing Your Library Services

Getting Started

What really gets your students excited? Have you asked them? Children today are more sophisticated in their ideas of what looks good. Television and video games make it difficult to compete for their attention. The most effective displays are those that have been designed with your students and reading program in mind from the beginning.

A big budget doesn't necessarily mean a successful display. It is possible with limited funds to create just the right motivation to draw in your students to check out books and want to read. Let your love for reading shine brightly through your displays and it will pay big dividends.

Even if you are not artistic, you can create great displays. Move beyond slapping up a few laminated reading posters. Be creative and try something new. Keep things simple at first but always keep materials looking fresh, clean, and colorful. Consider using lots of lights. Rope lights make great borders and create the feeling of a neon sign.

It is great to reuse items to create new displays, but, if the paper is faded, throw it out! Reading should be exciting and the displays must reflect energy and excitement—not faded and tired. Students already think we are old and out of touch. Imagine their surprise when you turn on the lights in a display for the first time and the action begins.

Patterns are included in this book which you can enlarge by using an opaque projector or copy machine. Use letter patterns, die-cut letters or computer generated words for your displays. Sloppy lettering really detracts from a display. Always check your spelling and punctuation because it is embarrassing when your students point out the mistakes. (And they will!)

Try to incorporate 3-D displays into your plans along with the old traditional bulletin boards. Look around the room or in the hallway for spaces you have never used before. How about the ceiling or that bottom book shelf you haven't been using? Get down on the floor and look at the room from the perspective of the first grader or stand on a chair and see what your really tall students are looking at.

Create a new space for a display by hanging up a clear shower curtain somewhere in the room. You can still see through it but it's a great space to hang posters, photographs, etc., or to serve as a divider in the room. Another idea is to use fishing line to hang a 4' × 8' sheet of foam insulation from the ceiling for a quick, portable bulletin board. You will soon discover many possible uses for this new display material.

Book displays can be set up virtually anywhere. Use the top of a bookshelf, a table top, a crate, a suitcase or trunk, a ladder, a wagon, or even a wheelbarrow. Change these displays often to correspond to special celebrations or school events.

Be sure to include time for maintenance. Even the best displays require some attention from time to time.

Each library is different and each population has different needs and requirements. Consider conducting a simple survey of your patrons. I recently surveyed the faculty in my school to help me in my plans for future displays and services. How would you answer the questions in the following survey?

Survey

Please answer the following questions based on your experiences using libraries, whether as a child or an adult.

1. When you hear the word "library," what images pop into your mind? (Good or bad)

2. What area of the library are you first drawn to? What usually captures your attention first?

3. Do you like to browse special displays or do you just skip them altogether?

4. When you were in elementary and high school, were you taught library skills? Were you instructed by the librarian?

5. Do you take the time to look at bulletin boards and other "decorations" when you are in the library? Do you think these are important?

6. When you walk into a store for the first time, what do you look for? Please number these in order of importance to you with #1 being the most important.

    ____   cleanliness

    ____   desired merchandise

    ____   arrangement and orderliness

    ____   friendliness and helpfulness of staff

    ____   signs and advertising

    ____   ease at the checkout—able to make the purchase quickly

The results I received interested me and have influenced some of my plans. The majority of my school faculty does browse special displays and feels that bulletin boards and "decorations" help make the library very inviting. Question 6 was answered with these results:

#1—desired merchandise

#2—arrangement

#3—cleanliness

#4—ease at checkout

#5—friendliness of staff

#6—signs and advertising

These responses will guide some of my future decisions. I view the library as a business that sells information and I want my library to be a very successful business.

Starting the Year in Style

The way you begin the school year can have an effect on the success of your program. Your enthusiasm will be contagious. Who should be more excited about your space and the joy of reading than you?

Keep things fresh and new in your library. Change things often—not the big things like the book shelves—just the arrangement of the tables, the color scheme, the posters, the pillow covers, etc. Look around your library or classroom and see what could use some sprucing up. If possible, touch up chipped paint anywhere in the room or just re-cover some of those tired cushions and pillows. Keep your students guessing. What will she do next? It's of the utmost importance that the students want to come to the library. After all, your library should be the center of the school's universe.

Quiet Reading Area

The stereotype of a librarian is one of a little old lady with her finger to her lips, saying "SHHH!" Although keeping the noise in the library to a minimum is a good idea, don't go overboard. Consider designating an area where only reading is permitted. This means no whispering, nothing but reading. Suggest to those who feel that they must talk that they should sit elsewhere. This requires your attention at first but the students will catch on very quickly and appreciate the quiet area.

This area might just be a rug with some pillows. A sofa and chairs would be awesome but they require a lot of room and can't be moved around easily. A baby bed mattress covered with fabric makes a great seating area on the floor. These can often be picked up at garage sales for not much money. Another teacher might just have one in the garage she would love to donate.

Computers

What about your computer area? Have you ever considered giving your computers names? So what if your students think you're a little crazy at first. It won't be long until they can't imagine how it was before the computers had names.

A name contest is a great way to get your students involved. The prize is that the winning name suggestion is used. Ex: The Big Bad Wolf, Cinderella, Little Red Riding Hood, Goldilocks, Shrek, or Tinkerbell. The name possibilities are endless. One good use for the names is that you will know exactly which computer a student is having a problem with. The student can tell you, "Goldilocks has an error message," and it is obvious which computer needs your attention. Depending on the number of computers you have available, this can be very helpful.

Paper and pencils are often hard to keep in supply in the computer area. Consider placing a flower pot or large basket of brightly colored plastic flowers in the area. These are really artificial flowers attached with floral tape to inexpensive ink pens. They are easy to create and not only do the children enjoy writing with them, they are also easy to spot leaving the area.

11

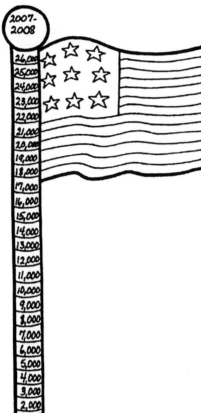

Circulation Statistics

Your patrons will enjoy knowing how many items are checked out from the library. Make a year-long visual display that tracks this checkout number.

Consider making a flag pole. This could be done on a support post in the room or along a piece of electrical conduit on a wall or just by using a long piece of paper for the pole. Use a fabric U.S. flag or a paper version. Be sure to follow all the rules of proper flag etiquette. Every time 1,000 books are checked out, move the flag up the pole. Another suggestion would be to posi-

tion the flag on a paper pole and just color in the pole as the checkout number increases.

A large thermometer made from poster paper or posterboard works well to display the checkout statistics. Use a red marker to color in the spaces as the number increases.

Another suggestion would be to make a silly smiley face drawn on

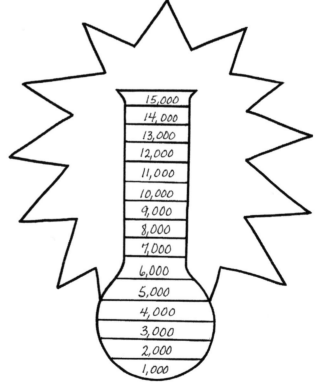

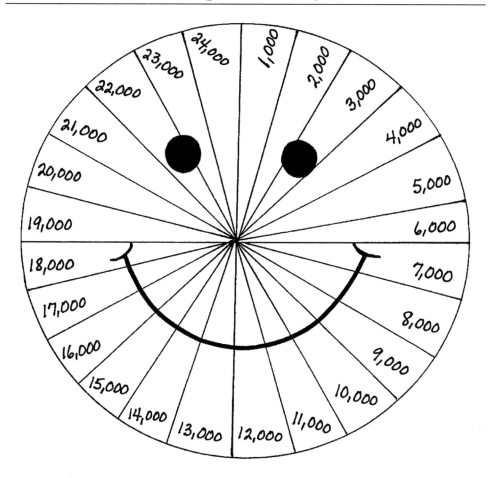

white posterboard. Begin with the largest circle you can possibly make on the piece of posterboard. Divide the circle into as many sections as you consider realistic for your library for the year. Put numbers such as 1,000, 2,000, and so on, in each space. Add two eyes and a large grin in black marker. To create a more finished design, mount the circle on another piece of poster board in a contrasting color.

Use a yellow marker to color in the spaces as the checkout number grows. If you complete the face and still need to add more, draw in hair, ears, etc. The children will enjoy the process and the end-of-the-year results.

Create excitement by giving prizes when some big milestones in circulation occur. The 10,000 mark is a great place to start, with 20,000, then 30,000 to soon follow. Prizes don't need to be expensive or elaborate. The best thing is to take a photograph of the winner and prominently display it.

Book Reviews

Often a student will come to the library and have difficulty choosing a book. One way to help is to have a notebook of student book reviews. Students are encouraged to fill out a book review form about a good book they have just read. The only rule is that the book reviewed must be a library book. Place the notebook in a readily accessible spot.

Book Review

Title_____

Author_____

Call #_____

Level/Points_____
(include if your school has a reading program)

Type of book_____
(mystery, ghost story, adventure, horse story, travel, history, animal story, etc.)

In this book. . . . . . . ._____

_____

_____

_____

_____

_____

_____

_____

I would recommend this book because. . . . . . _____

_____

_____

_____

_____

_____

_____

_____
Name

Library Passes

In the school setting, library passes are a must. Begin the year by preparing passes for each classroom. If your school has a theme for the year, design your passes to support the theme. Regardless of the design you choose, you will need to put the teacher's name on the pass and the word "library." Laminate these if possible to lengthen their lifespan.

Consider creating VIP passes. These are special passes for students as a reward to allow them to come to the library on their own to just relax and read. The pass could be for thirty minutes or at the discretion of the child's teacher. This library "free time" could be a valuable commodity.

Communication

Keep the lines of communication open between parents and the library. One easy way to help the parents of kindergarten students get into your library's routine is to send a note home each time a child forgets to return a book. Create a form that fits your needs and just fill in the title of the book that was not returned. This takes almost no time and parents do appreciate the information. This is an example:

Dear Parent:

Your child came to the library today for library time with their class. Your child was not able to check out a book today because he/she has not yet returned the following book:

_____

Each kindergarten student is permitted to check out one book at a time. Please feel free to keep the book a few days longer if you are not finished reading it with your child. Your child may check out a new book as soon as this one has been returned.

If you have any questions concerning your child and the library, please feel free to contact me during school hours at 498–4036.

Mrs. Skaggs, Librarian

Communication with your faculty is really important. Get their input on library purchase suggestions. Teachers may not always think to discuss new units or projects with you. Take the initiative and ask how you can help them. They many think you are very pushy at first, but they will quickly catch on and will soon begin asking for the moon. The squeaky wheel gets the oil!

Communication with your administration is vital. You should be the most vocal advocate for your library. Keep the administration informed of your library's needs. They probably share your goal of creating the best library possible but they are relying on you to know what is needed and to inform them of these needs. Be wise and be vocal.

A Library Introduction Project

A great project to begin the year for students in grades 2–4 is to create a map of the library. This is a great opportunity for students to ask questions and begin the year learning where everything in the library is located. Draw off a simple floor plan indicating shelves, computers, and checkout desk without any type of labeling. Copy these, providing one to each child. Have each child bring a pencil and crayons to the library. As you explain each part of the library, the children will color in and label the areas. Designate a color code such as blue for the nonfiction shelves, red for fiction chapter books, green for easy fiction, etc. Be sure to have a legend or map key included with the main areas listed and a small box the children can color in for the color designation of that specific area.

When completed, these maps are "treasure maps." They will help your students to discover many of the great treasures that your library has to offer.

Doin' the Dewey

Our goal is to help our students to be independent users of the library. What a joy to see a child search the card catalog and after finding the call number, go to the shelf and find the book for himself. What a feeling of accomplishment!

Teaching the Dewey Decimal System doesn't mean that the lessons will be boring. This is not something that is out-of-date but is instead a wonderful organizational system that can work into every lesson. After a basic or simple explanation of the system, send the students on a treasure hunt. The treasure they will search for are call numbers. Just write two or three call numbers on a white board or chalkboard and send students out on the hunt. This works so well for second and third grade students and they will beg to look for them.

To begin your presentation of the Dewey Decimal System (DDS), create a focal point with a simple eye-catching display using rope lights for a border. A background of yellow paper and bright red letters will be very attention-getting.

When your first through third grade classes come in for some library time, plan to read a fiction book and a nonfiction book on the same topic. For example, to showcase the 500s, read *Diary of a Worm* and a nonfiction book on earthworms. A little dirt and some real worms or night crawlers would spice up the lesson.

A suggestion for the 600s would be to showcase the exercise books and those on bones, muscles, and good eating habits. Do some exercises with your students right there in the library. *Mousercize* is a great resource for this.

The 700s is a fantastic opportunity to do some drawing. Pick a drawing

MELVIL DEWEY

The man with the plan!

book and follow the directions to draw something on the chalkboard (white board) while the children draw on paper. This is a good chance to talk about following directions and most children love to draw.

Create postcards after a lesson with your travel books. Four by six inch white construction paper or card stock works well for this. Hang these in the library or in the hall. Help students put the correct Dewey number on their postcard for the book's address.

Dewey Games

Another way to ease into the DDS is through games. Use every opportunity to call attention to these areas and the kind of books in each.

MATCH GAME

Create a matching game by printing two copies of each of the Dewey numbers and area titles onto card stock.

Example: 000   200   500
                General Works   Religion   Science

Cut these into squares and laminate. The game is played by laying out all of the pieces upside down. Students take turns trying to make a match. If the child is successful in making a match, he or she continues. The game goes on until all the matches are made.

CHECK-IT-OUT GAME

A card game similar to Go Fish is really popular with elementary students. On 52 3 × 5 blank index cards, use markers to make the game pieces. You will need four of each of the following:

000 General Works   700 The Arts
100 Philosophy/Psychology   800 Literature
200 Religion   900 History
300 Social Science   910–919 Geography
400 Language   92 Biography
500 Science   Fiction
600 Technology (or Useful Arts)

You will probably need to use markers on the back of each card create some type of colorful design. This is to keep one from seeing what is on the other side of the card. The marker may show through. Whatever design you choose, repeat it on all 52 cards to have a matched deck. Vary the design for each deck of cards you create. One deck works well for four students to play the game. If possible, laminate the cards to lengthen their life span. Make as many sets as needed for the size of your class.

To play, the dealer gives each student in the game seven cards. The remaining cards are placed in a stack in the center of the table. The player to the left of the dealer goes first and asks another player—for example—"May I please have all of your 200s Religion?" The student who has been asked this checks his cards and relinquishes all the 200s as requested. If he does not have a 200, he says "check-it-out." The player who made the request must draw a card from the top of the pile. If the card drawn was the number he had been asking for, his turn continues. The goal is to collect four of the same

Dewey number and this is called a "book." When a player runs out of cards, the game is over. The one with the most books is the winner.

Encourage the students to say not only the number, but also the Dewey area title when they are playing the game. The purpose of the game is to help the children associate the number and the Dewey title.

PUZZLES

Most libraries have some of those old posters that depict the items in the various Dewey sections. These make great puzzles. Cut them into pieces and store each in its own envelope. These work well to capture the attention of those students who finish checking out ahead of their classmates.

BINGO

Another popular Dewey game is based on Bingo. Print off cards that say DEWEY with a small "1" by the first "E" and a "2" by the second "E." There is no free space on the card. You will need to write in the numbers so that all of the cards will be different. Cut small pieces of construction paper to use as markers or use beans, etc. (The problem with paper markers is that they are easily blown off.)

D	E^1	W	E^2	Y

Print one of each of the following:

D	General Works	D	Science
D	Philosophy/Psychology	D	Technology
D	Religion	D	The Arts
D	Social Science	D	Literature
D	Language	D	History

Do this for "E1," "W," "E2," and "Y." Cut these apart and put them in a basket, box, or bag. These are what will be drawn and called out when playing the game.

To begin the game, give each student a list of the Dewey numbers and the associated word for each. After playing the game for a while, collect these lists. The students will have to rely on their memory. Call out only the words and they will have to fill in the spot on their Bingo cards for the correct number.

During the game use a chalkboard to list each Dewey area called. This allows the students to keep up and is a way to refer to what has been called. This is also the place to check when a student thinks he or she has a Bingo. Have them read off what they have marked on their card as you check the chalkboard.

It is fun to play five in a row horizontally, vertically, or diagonally. After the first student gets a Bingo, try "blackout," which means that every space must be filled.

Fourth Grade Dewey Decimal System Unit

After introducing the Dewey Decimal System and pointing out the various areas in the library, divide the class (grade) into 13 groups—one for each Dewey area plus biography. The 300s (300–379 and 380–399) and 500s (500–569 and 570–599) should be split into two groups each because they are such large areas in your library. Divide other areas as needed.

Assign a Dewey area to each group. The students will work in this same group for two projects.

PROJECT 1—LARGE POSTER

The project is to create a poster that will "sell" a particular Dewey area.

Provide posterboard or large sheets of white paper so that the posters will be uniform in size.

The group should spend time at the shelves taking notes on the kinds of books in their assigned Dewey number. Encourage the group to brainstorm. The poster should include drawings to illustrate the Dewey area. For example: The 700s could include baseball bats, footballs, a skateboard, fishing poles, artist supplies, music notes, cartoons, etc. The Dewey number should be prominently displayed along with the name of the area. Crayons, colored pencils, markers, or cut and glued construction paper would be great.

This project may take two or three class periods. Hang these in the library or the hallway nearest the library. If possible, invite the groups to come and share their information about the Dewey system with another grade or class.

PROJECT 2—DEWEY DECIMAL SYSTEM COMMERCIAL

Working in the same groups as before and with the same Dewey area as for the poster, the students will write, act, and film commercials. These could even be done as a PowerPoint presentation if you have those technology options available. Encourage the children to be creative. Each group is now an advertising agency and the library is its client. Talk about the different types of commercials and possibly show a few as examples. Ask them what their favorite commercials are and why they are effective or ineffective.

Create a handout that specifies your requirements for this project. Set dates and stick with them. Work with the classroom teacher to correlate this project with the grade's communication arts objectives. An example of this handout follows.

Each group is responsible for creating a commercial but is also responsible for filming for another group. This is an opportunity for the students to work with a video camera and stopwatch. Using two video cameras is suggested, as occasionally the cameraman may not have been recording when he thought he was. Have a meeting with the groups prior to filming to go over all the details. Planning is a must.

After the commercials have been filmed, copy the best from each group onto a master tape and plan a big "Dewey" celebration similar to the Oscars. Take a still photo of each group and create some publicity posters.

Advertise the event and be sure to have a red carpet and lots of balloons. Provide bubblegum to ease the tension, as there will be lots of nervous excitement. Chewing on that gum really helps! The more excited your are, the more excited they will be.

Invite the 5th grade to be "The Academy" to view the completed commercials and choose the winners. Before the showing, remind these students of the awesome responsibility they have been given. Give simple prizes such as candy to the winners of such categories as:

Most Humorous	Most Creative
Most Educational	Best Commercial of All

Dewey Decimal Commercial

You will work in the same group as you did on the poster and will be working with the same area of the Dewey Decimal System. Each person in the group is responsible for working on the commercial. Each person in the group must be in the commercial.

REQUIREMENTS

1. The commercial should be designed to encourage people to want to check out books from that particular Dewey Decimal area. The purpose of a commercial is to sell something—in this case, a particular type of book.

2. The commercial must be at least 30 seconds but no more than 45 seconds long.

3. Props and costumes may be used but they must be provided by the group.

4. A written script must be given to the librarian on or before the day of taping. Each group will have a pre-taping conference with the librarian and the group that will be filming them.

5. Each group will be producing a commercial and working to film another group.

6. The technical crew for each commercial will be:

   2 cameramen

   1 time keeper

   1 director

7. There will only be two "takes" for each group. This means that there are only two chances for the group to get the commercial right.

COMMENTS

I had parents calling me to see what time the commercials would be on television. We were maybe just a little too excited!

After the project was completed, I had students in both the 4th and 5th grades coming in looking for books in areas they had never considered before. We had a commercial for the 000s in which aliens were playing basketball trying to get in the *Guiness Book of World Records.* Another for the 800s included a babysitting service, quoted poetry and had a 1–800 phone number. This continues to be a very successful project year after year.

Other Curriculum Suggestions

When you hear the word "library," what images immediately pop into your head? Hopefully, they are great images of favorite books or stories read to you as a child rather than the face of a crabby librarian telling you to be quiet. We don't realize that everything we do for our patrons is creating a memory of the library—good or bad.

Our goal is to create independent users of the library. Information and the ability to find and use information is very powerful. I believe that confidence building in improving library skills will lead to a desire to use the library more often. How can we help our patrons to develop the information skills necessary for today's world? The following are some curricular suggestions and activities to help children to grow in library skills. This is not a complete list but just basic suggestions that should be a part of any library skills program. Present new skills each year and build on those presented in previous years. Skills can be reviewed just by changing the activity.

Kindergarten/First Grade

I. Orientation
    A. Knows the location of the library and can recognize the library staff.
        Take a photograph of the librarian standing in the library doorway. Post this in the kindergarten and first grade classrooms for the first

weeks of school with the message. "Our class visits Mrs. Skaggs in the library on Wednesdays."

B. Learns circulation routine for borrowing and returning books.

Read *Stella Luella's Runaway Book*. Talk about your library's circulation policies along with tips about keeping the books clean and away from younger siblings and pets. Focus on the positives of checking out a book rather than the consequences.

C. Knows that materials in the library have a specific order and understands his own part in keeping materials in order.

Demonstrate the use of shelf markers. Shelf markers can be as simple as paint stir sticks or can be purchased from library vendors. Provide a cart where books can be placed for reshelving if the student does not know the correct spot on the shelf to return the book.

II. Literature Appreciation

A. Becomes familiar with well-known authors and illustrators.

Choose an author who has a birthday during the month and read several of his or her books. Have the children talk about the books, comparing and contrasting them. Does the author use the same character in more than one book? Does the artwork of the illustrator look similar from book to book or is each book very different? Go to the shelves and show the location of this author's books. Show a photo of the author and tell the students a little about the author's life. Set up a small display of books by this author to encourage the children to read more on their own. Refer back to this author during the year to help the children to remember him or her.

B. Knows that some books receive special awards, e.g. the Caldecott medal.

Children love the gold seals on the covers of award winning books. Many times children excitedly check out a book because "it is a winner!" Read several Caldecott books with different types of artwork—pencil drawings, ink drawings, chalk, paintings, etc. Ask the children about their preferences. Display Caldecott books in January near the time the new winner is announced. Many book companies provide free posters depicting the covers of all of the Caldecott winners.

C. Is familiar with different types of literature, including multicultural and ethnic literature.

Display many simple poetry books. Read poems about school, food, little brothers and sisters, etc. *Giant Children* is full of funny poems. Be sure to read some "gross" ones. Point out where the 800s are located and while you are there, throw in a joke and riddle.

Read many culturally different versions of *Cinderella*. There are over 1500 versions. Have the children tell you the differences from and similarities to the Disney version they know. There are a vast number of lesson plans on the Internet for a study of *Cinderella*. These are some of the versions you might pick from: *Yeh-Shen, Cinderella Penguin, Cinderella Bigfoot, Prince Cinders, Princess Furball, Egyptian Cinderella, Korean Cinderella, Rough-Face Girl, Cinder Edna, Sootface, Raisel's Riddle, Ashpet: an Appalachian Tale, Moss Gown, Mufaro's Beautiful Daughters, The Golden Slipper, The Enchanted Anklet, Sidney Rella and the Glass Sneaker, Cinderlad, Rufferella, Queen of the May, The Talking Eggs, The Starlight Cloak, Tattercoats. Vasilisa the Beautiful, When the Nightingale Sings, Wishbones, The Turkey Girl, Nomi and the Magic Fish, Lily and the Wooden Bowl, Little Firefly, Dinorella, Smoky Mountain Rose, and Slender Ella and Her Fairy Hogfather.*

This Cinderella unit works well with all grade levels. Consider a lesson from the stepsister's point of view.

III. Organization/Listening, Reading and Viewing Skills

A. Learns the difference between fiction and nonfiction and how to locate each type.

Choose a subject and then read a short fiction and nonfiction book on that subject. Talk about the differences and where each type is located in the library. Ex: *The Frog Principal* and *Fabulous Fantastic Rainforest Tree Frogs*.

B. Develops the ability to attend to sights and sounds of storytelling.

Consider telling a story to the children rather than reading one. "The Gnome in the Peanut" from *The Orphan Annie Storybook* is a great story to tell. Do not show any pictures. Let the children use their imaginations.

C. Develops visual literacy skills.

Share a book such as *Tuesday* (David Wiesner). This book, which has flying frogs on lily pads, is just awesome, not to mention that it is a Caldecott winner. Allow the children to help you tell the story, making it as personal as possible. This book has almost no words.

D. Can relate story to own experiences and state the main idea of a story or passage.

Read a story about a dog or cat. *A Dog Like Jack* or *Go Home* are good examples. Most children have a cat or dog story to share.

Second/Third Grade

I. Orientation

A. Can locate and identify major areas of the library.

Create a map of the library as described previously in the "Starting the Year in Style" chapter.

II. Organization

A. Is familiar with the card catalog and can locate a book by author, title, or subject.

The librarian explains or reviews the use of the electronic card catalog. The students demonstrate their knowledge by using the catalog to find materials for a classroom project.

B. Uses alphabetical order by the first three letters of the author's last name.

A stack of assorted fiction books are put on each table. The children work as a group to put them in order. Repeat the process by moving the children to different tables.

C. Knows the difference between fiction and nonfiction and how to locate each type.

After a careful explanation of the call number information on the label of the book, the children work in groups to sort 10 to 15 books. The books are put in order by call number with fiction and nonfiction in separate piles.

D. Practices and reviews the Dewey Decimal System.

Play Dewey games such as those suggested in the chapter, "Doin' the Dewey."

Focus on activities that feature each area of the Dewey System. One of my favorite ones is for the 500s. Read a story about tongues. Animals have all different shapes and sizes of tongues. Give the students magnifying glasses to use to look at each other's tongues. This is fun but very educational. They will remember the 500s!

The 700s offer a wonderful opportunity to teach a lesson on following directions. Use a "how to draw" book and read the directions, going step by step as you help the children draw something. This is important to help the child develop good listening skills and to value directions. The finished drawings are just a bonus!

III. Selection, Interpretation, Evaluation

A. Can interpret information from simple maps and charts.

Use a large world map to point out the locations in a story read to the class. Always show the locations relative to your school's location. Ex. *Ben's Dream* (Chris Van Allsburg). Use Post-it notes to mark the locations on the map as the story progresses.

Use the map in the local telephone book to introduce and reinforce map skills.

Use your state's road maps to teach students the grid method of finding locations on a map. Pair the children up and spread them out as they search for cities and towns in your state. Contact your state highway department for maps.

B. Can select appropriate fiction or subject area in nonfiction for their particular interest.

Allow the students to choose freely in your library. I believe that it is okay for the child to choose something that is too difficult every once in awhile. Many times they are just drawn to the pictures and reading the pictures may just be the beginning of something really big.

IV. Reference Skills

A. Can use a dictionary to find meanings of unknown words. Introduce the unabridged dictionary.

Each time a word is used in a story that the students do not understand, the word is looked up in a dictionary to demonstrate and reinforce the process.

   B. Can use the telephone directory as a source of information.

      The librarian presents the telephone book as a useful reference tool. Guide words are stressed along with the different types of information included. The similarities of the dictionary are pointed out with practice given in locating telephone numbers, zip codes, items in the Yellow Pages, etc.

   C. Can use encyclopedias to find needed information, whether in print or online.

V. Book/Non-Book Format

   A. Can identify parts of a book: cover, spine, label, author, title, table of contents, glossary, index, publisher, copyright date, place of publication.

      Each student is given a book to look at as the librarian leads a discussion of these book parts.

   B. Becomes familiar with periodical format and—location of periodicals in the library.

      Students are permitted to look at magazines during any free time and are encouraged to use online periodicals. As an activity, an assortment of periodicals are put on each table. The students look at them as the librarian points out the features such as the date, title, and table of contents.

VI. Literature Appreciation

   A. Knows the parts of a story—narrator, plot, setting, character—and can summarize what happens in a story.

      Read a story and then lead a discussion that includes comparing and contrasting story characters.

   B. Be introduced to and use biographies and autobiographies.

      February is Black History Month. Encourage the children to read a book about a famous African American.

      During the World Series, encourage the children to read a biography of a famous baseball player—or do the same during the Super Bowl time with your football biographies.

Fourth Grade

Continue building on previous skills by changing to more difficult activities.

I. Reference Skills

A. Understands the Dewey Decimal System.

Do projects outlined in the "Doin' the Dewey" chapter. This unit may take two or three months and includes making posters and filming commercials. This is definitely a collaborative project between the classroom teacher and the librarian.

B. Can locate and use a biographical and geographical dictionary.

C. Can recognize parts of a newspaper.

Students are encouraged to read the newspaper in the library and online.

D. Can locate an almanac and find information in it.

II. Selection, Interpretation, Evaluation

A. Can interpret information from time lines, tables, diagrams, and graphs.

This skill can be practiced as students explore and use the almanac.

B. Can interpret information from maps and charts.

Use atlases to teach about political, physical, and thematic maps. Have the students use the index to locate various cities, towns, countries, rivers, etc. Discuss how you could make a map to represent a particular idea such as poverty, extreme temperatures, etc.

I recommend that the first day the atlas is used be called "the gawking day." This is a time for the students to look at everything in the atlas they want to see. Believe me, they will do it anyway when you are trying to teach your lesson, so get it out of the way right off the bat!

C. Can choose appropriate reference books for a given task.

After a discussion of the reference books, each student is given a person or place to research. The student is required to use two to three sources to accomplish the project.

Fifth/Sixth Grade

I. Organization

A. Knows the main classes of the Dewey Decimal System.

Students play Nerf basketball. Students are divided into two teams. One student from the first team shoots the Nerfball at the basket. If a basket is made, the student is shown a Dewey area number. He must name a type of book found in that area. Two points are given for a correct answer. If the student cannot answer, his team is given an opportunity to answer. The play alternates between the two teams. The team with the most points at the end of the allotted time wins.

II. Reference Skills

A. Can locate and use biographical, geographical, unabridged, visual, and foreign language dictionaries.

The class is divided into five groups. Each group is assigned one of the above types of dictionary. The group reviews the books and then presents the information to the class. Note-taking sheets are provided.

B. Can select a volume of an encyclopedia to locate a topic.

The differences in the sets of encyclopedias are reviewed—general and specialized. The importance of the index is stressed.

C. Can locate an almanac and find information in it.

Students will work through "World Almania" bootcamp to develop skills in keyword searches, understanding the three indexes, search strategies, etc. The students take part in "World Almania" competition (5th grade vs. 6th grade). "World Almania" is a teaching tool developed for use with *The World Almanac*. This whole process will take at least two months. (The game is very much like the Jeopardy game but you do not have to know the answer, just be able to find the answer very quickly in the almanac.)

D. Can locate and use a book of quotations.

Using *Bartlett's Familiar Quotations,* students must find a quotation on a particular subject.

III. Selection, Interpretation, Evaluation

A. Can interpret information from maps and charts.

   Pair up students and give each team a road map from somewhere in the United States. The two students must work together to plan a trip to a location on their assigned map. They must determine distance from your school, population of the destination, the best roads to take to get there, time needed for travel, etc. This is just practice in using the map keys, estimation, and related skills.

B. Can check validity and reliability of sources by comparing information from more than one source, including periodicals.

C. Can synthesize information, bringing parts together into a meaningful whole.

   After consulting many sources, students will be able to complete a report on an assigned topic.

D. Interprets intended meaning from a source.

   The librarian reads a passage from some literary form followed by a class discussion. Ex. *The Raven*.

E. Develop search strategies, e.g. Boolean.

   The librarian demonstrates this search technique for the electronic media with plenty of time given for exploration.

Seventh/Eighth Grade

By this level, it should be a continuation of skills lessons with the majority of emphasis on mastery of research skills. Students often have a difficult time understanding the concept that the word "research" means "re"—do again and again—and "search"—looking for something. Research requires effort and often a good deal of time. These skills are generally worked on as needed in cooperation with the course instructor.

Puppetry in the Library

Puppets have been in use for centuries. They have a certain appeal for people of all ages. Many times people will listen to what a puppet has to say when they wouldn't consider listening otherwise. Puppets could add a new dimension to your library services.

You could approach the use of puppets in two ways. One way would be for you and your staff, if you are fortunate to have others working with you, to present puppet shows for your patrons. Keep the shows short and simple. This is a great way to tell a story through skits and songs.

Another option is to form a puppet team of interested students and have them do the presentations. This is a wonderful opportunity to help students develop leadership skills and learn to work as a team. In recruiting your team, have some requirements. I believe that it is important that the students must commit to maintaining a particular grade point average while they are a member of the team. This should be at least what is required by your school for participation in athletics. This is hard work, so you will need committed puppeteers.

Puppets

Puppets come in all shapes and sizes. Hand puppets are the most common and marionettes are the most complex. Puppets can be purchased from countless sources or may be handmade. Consider a variety of animals and people. Because it is actually more important for "people" puppets to be more believable than animal puppets, it is often best to use professionally produced people puppets.

The correct way to operate a puppet is to position the hand in the puppet's mouth by putting the four fingers in the roof of the mouth and the thumb in the jaw area. The lower jaw drops during speech but the upper lip does not go up. This is difficult at first but can be accomplished with practice.

To strengthen your arm and to hone your technique, stand in a doorway and extend your arm so that your hand touches the top of the doorjamb. Stand on a chair or stool if you need to do so to reach the top. Practice moving only the thumb while keeping the four fingers pressed against the top of the doorjamb.

A common mistake by new puppeteers is to bite words. This means that the puppeteer closes the puppet's mouth with each word instead of opening the mouth for the word. It is also not necessary for the puppet to attempt to speak every syllable of a word. Practice by having your puppet sing along with some prerecorded music or practice mouthing while listening to television. Your puppet needs to become a lipsync champion.

The way the puppets enter and exit is also very important. Pretend to walk the puppet up a staircase. To exit, just reverse the process. Do not instantly appear or disappear.

There are two kinds of hand puppets. The most common are puppets with arms that are manipulated with rods. However, there are puppets which allow you to use your hands. These human-hand puppets provide the opportunity to hold props, pretend to play musical instruments, gesture, etc. Often two people work together to manipulate a human-hand puppet. One person operates the mouth while the other wears gloves and does the puppet's hands. This is a more advanced technique but it is very effective and attention-getting.

Allow lots of time for practice. Children are much more sophisticated concerning visual presentations than they were twenty years ago. They are accustomed to seeing puppets on shows such as *Sesame Street* and they will unconsciously compare. Practice, practice, practice!

Show Suggestions

Whenever possible use prerecorded material, whether skits or songs. If you are writing your own material, record it for the performance. It is difficult to manipulate a puppet well and speak a part at the same time. There are often times when you might develop a cough or one of the regular performers is absent. A pre-recorded program eliminates the hassle.

Puppet Productions is an excellent source of puppets and puppet skits. It is available on the Web, as are other great companies. Skits are available on health and safety issues along with character education topics such as bullying, accepting responsibility and honesty.

Songs are great to start with as you strive to become a better puppeteer. Disney's *Silly Songs* and *More Silly Songs* are wonderful. Its song "Cupcakes and Lemonade" is the story of Little Red Riding Hood and it is just awesome to use in a puppet presentation. *Veggie Tale* CDs offer many great songs, too, such as "Consider Yourself Part of the Family" and "A Friend is a Friend." Or how about "Flight of the Bumblebee" done with an animal such as a lion and a pesky bumblebee?

Keep your eyes and ears open for show material. Be creative!

Puppetry Suggestions

1. Do not overact with your puppet. The goal is to have your puppet appear as human as possible.

2. If you do not feel confident using rods to control the puppet's hands, just let them hang. Often the arms are in a distorted position when the rods are not used correctly.

3. Do not allow your puppet to be a show stealer. Every puppet should be a team player in order for there to be a successful production.

4. Be sure the puppet's mouth is closed when the puppet isn't talking.

5. Keep the puppet's nose down so that the audience can see the puppet's eyes.

6. Don't allow the puppets to be seen outside the stage. This destroys the magic.

7. Don't lean on the stage! It is so embarrassing when it falls down!

Stages

A stage can be very simple or as elaborate as you want to make it. A simple stage can be one hung in a doorway. This stage can be taken down and folded for storage. Use two tension rods and fabric to create a stage for one or possibly two people to use. This can be made from scraps of fabric that don't even match well. Use bold colors that are plain, polka dot, striped, flowered or even plaid. They need to be "kid appealing" colors.

Make a casing in the top of a rectangle of fabric that is the width of the doorway. A casing is just two seams that are about an inch apart. Insert a tension rod. Sew on two strips of fabric to form the sides of the performance area.

Connect the two strips to another piece of fabric that is the width of the doorway and that can reach the floor when hung. Create a casing to insert the second tension rod. Add extra details such as little curtains.

For a larger team of puppeteers, consider making a stage from PVC pipe. This type of stage can easily be disassembled for travel or storage. (This stage is the "Cadillac" model but will last for many years.)

Below is a suggested size stage for approximately six puppeteers with a top and bottom stage area. The size can be adjusted to fit your needs.

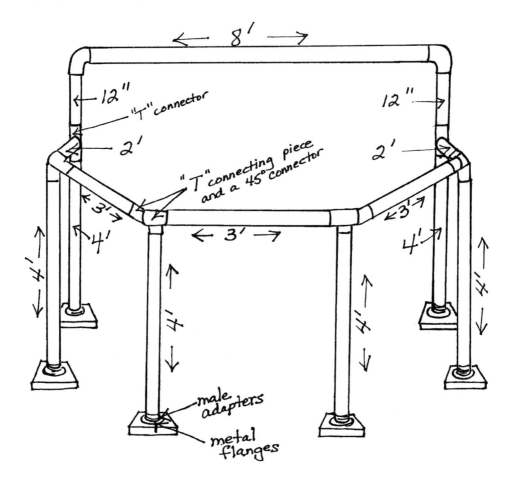

Materials needed:
Use PVC pipe that is 1½" (or 1¹/₄" for a lighter weight stage)
6 pieces of pipe 4' in length
1 piece of pipe 8' in length
2 pieces of pipe 2' in length
3 pieces of pipe 3' in length
2 pieces of pipe 12" in length

6 metal flanges to hold 1½" pipe

6 1½" male adapters (to screw pipe into metal flanges)

2 elbow pieces

6 T connecting pieces

4 45° connectors

6 pieces of wood 9" square, 1" thick for the bases

4 pieces of pipe 2" in length

Fabric for the curtains.

PVC pipe can easily be cut with a hand saw. Lightly sand the edges to eliminate rough spots. See the design to determine the placement of each piece. Use a 2" piece of pipe to connect a T connector and a 45° connector. If necessary, use glue to permanently connect these pieces. This configuration allows your stage to be constructed with angles rather than just a square box design.

The curtain itself can be made from any fabric that blocks the light but doesn't wrinkle badly. It could even be made from old sheets. A casing needs to be sewn along the top to slide the curtain onto the pipes. A space needs to be left open at each connection point to allow you to connect the pipes together. To fit the bottom stage as shown in the drawing, use 9½ yards of fabric. This allows for plenty of fabric that gathers nicely.

The top stage is 8' long so purchase 2 yards of fabric that matches the bottom stage material or at least complements it, and cut along the fold to have two pieces of fabric that are each 2 yards long. Sew these together so that you have a strip that is now 4 yards long. Sew a casing that is large enough for a piece of pipe to slide through along one edge. If necessary, make a small hem along the other edge. Slide this onto the 8' pipe. An elbow piece goes on each end of the pipe and this will help to keep the curtain in place, besides connecting the pipe to the rest of the stage. Make a simple bag to store the stage pieces in. This can be made out of any old fabric. Because the 8' pole is so long, this will be a cumbersome thing to move around, but at least all the pieces will be together.

Part II

Marketing Through Displays and Reading Themes

The U.S.A.

With the implementation of reading programs such as Accelerated Reader and Reading Counts, many librarians are in the position of coordinating and cheerleading the program for their school. It isn't easy to come up with a theme that is appealing to your teachers and students and to maintain enthusiasm for a whole school year. For the first year, choose a simple topic that everyone can relate to, such as "The U.S.A."

The U.S.A. theme has so many possibilities that even those children who need a lot of extra motivation will find something to spark their interest. The theme was developed for use primarily with the Reading Counts or Accelerated Reader programs, but could easily be adapted for others. Although all the ideas might not be original, they are a collection of suggested activities to make the educator's job much easier.

Bulletin Boards and Displays

Patriotism is very important in our world today. The colors red, white, and blue are everywhere. Use these to your advantage with a theme such as "I'm proud to be an all–American reader" or "Celebrate your right to read." Flags, pennants, and red, white, and blue bunting are available in almost all party supply stores and discount stores. Put these up to begin the year and since they are not seasonal items, leave them up as long as you wish.

To start the first week of school with a bang, consider a temporary display that uses balloons to create a flag. This will take quite a bit of wall space and should probably not be in a high traffic area.

Use some painter's tape to set the perimeter of your flag. You determine the size that will work best for you. It's fine if you don't have the exact number of stripes in your balloon flag as a real U.S. flag but try to get as close as possible. Blow up plenty of red, white, and blue balloons that are all the same size and if possible, purchase blue balloons that have stars printed on them. Position the balloons in rows by sticking each of them to the wall with a piece of rolled-up tape or some double-sided tape. Remove the painter's tape after the flag is completed.

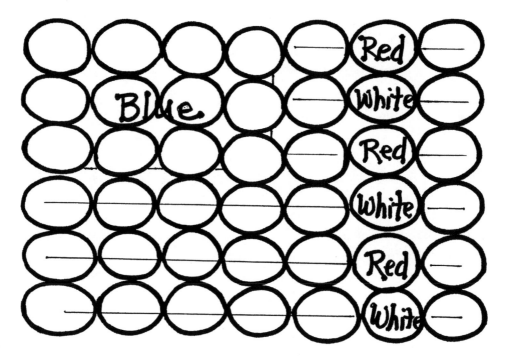

Don't forget the area around the door to your library. If the space permits, this area can also become a flag. Look at your available space. Divide it up with an area of dark blue paper and stripes of red and white poster paper. Cover the outside of the door as if it is part of the wall. Let it blend in to the flag design. Cut out the door window with a matte knife and trim the paper so that the door can open easily without catching.

Hang the stars with fishing line over the blue area of the display. Use black construction paper letters for your slogan.

Trust me, you will receive many compliments on your efforts.

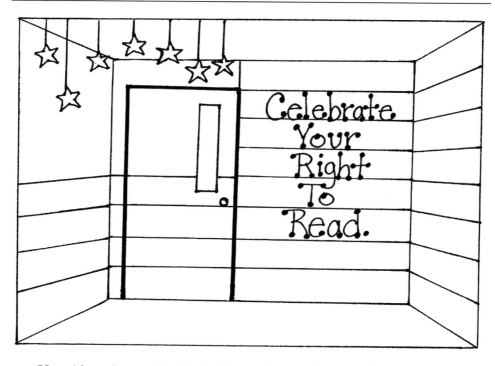

Use old road maps for the background cover for your bulletin boards. Covering boxes in these maps also works well in book displays. To fill an empty wall space, just cut large letters for the word "READ" from some old maps. Arrange them vertically or horizontally to best fit your space.

Create a display to chart your circulation statistics as the children enjoy watching the yearly number grow. Consider the idea of a flag pole as described in the "Starting the Year in Style" chapter.

Road signs and license plates add color and authenticity to your displays. A picture of each state's license plate can be found in the *World Almanac for*

Kids. Choose some to photocopy and enlarge. Add some color with markers and use these to mark the various Dewey areas on your shelves. Use a marker to put in the license number such as 000s, 100s, etc., or use subject areas such as "Mysteries" or Drawing Books."

Choose some well known tourist spots such as the Statue of Liberty, Niagara Falls, or the Grand Canyon or some big cities like New York, Los Angeles, or Dallas. Use www.ask.com to find the distances in miles between your town and these spots. Make road signs and place them around your library or throughout the school.

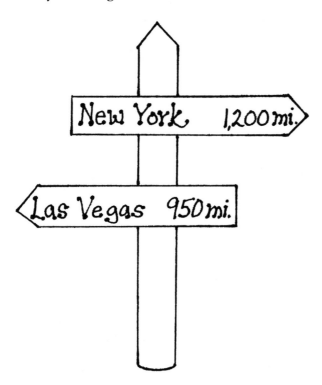

Children seem to love to work on word search puzzles. www.puzzle-maker.com allows you to make wonderful puzzles to supplement your U.S.A. theme. The subject possibilities are endless. Consider making puzzles of state names, U.S. cities, tourist areas, national parks, baseball teams, basketball teams, football teams, U.S. presidents, famous Americans.

Over the course of the year, display books from many different time periods and aspects of American life. These are just a few suggestions: Frontier and pioneer life, Native Americans, Cowboys, the '50s with rock and roll, Regions of the country—New England, the South, the Southwest, the Midwest, the Atlantic states, the Northwest, or The Pacific, great American inventions, and American holidays.

Wall Charts

To support your school's reading program, consider creating some type of wall chart to keep the children focused on reading. It is important to have something visual for the children to see as they progress to their reading goal. This can be done by creating a school-wide chart or individual classroom charts. Both are great and can be done well at the same time.

A school-wide chart helps to create ownership of the program and the goal by the children. Excitement builds as the chart or display moves to a completed state. The emphasis becomes one that every student is important and must do their part to complete the picture.

Creating a giant U.S. flag makes an awesome school-wide progress chart. The flag is made up of small squares of construction paper. Each square represents a particular point value, or however your reading program operates. Choose a large wall that is highly visible. Do some quick math with the dimensions and figure out how much space can be allotted for those thirteen stripes and just how big the blue area should be.

Next, determine what the size of each square should be. Four inch squares work well. Assign colors to specific classes or grades. For example, red for grades 1 and 2, white for grades 3 and 4, and blue for grades 5 and 6. Have the squares all cut from construction paper and cut a large amount to stockpile. You will use more than you could ever imagine.

The child writes his or her name on the square plus the number of points, such as 10, 20, 30, etc., and the date and whatever other pertinent information you deem necessary.

Designate one person to become the caretaker of the wall to insure a consistent look in the display. Maintenance needs to be included in the plans also.

Provide a drop-off basket or bag in the library for the completed squares. Your positive

remarks to the child when he or she drops off a square encourages him to keep up the good work. Hang up the squares each day because the children will check on them and the squares tend to add up quickly.

The first fifty students to reach their goal each get to put a white star on the flag. Being one of the first fifty is prestigious. Each child should receive a star when they have met their goal but only the first fifty go on the flag. Create another design somewhere else with these additional stars.

To give the flag a more three dimensional look, hang the fifty stars in front of the blue area in a staggered arrangement. Use fishing line to hang these stars from the ceiling. The fishing line becomes transparent and does not detract from the display. This gives the appearance of students being a part of the display because they can walk under the stars. Another benefit is that no child's blue square is covered up by a star.

Next to the flag hang an explanation of the colors, and other elements. Parents are very interested in a project such as this and it is important that they understand the significance of each element. Hang an additional sign when the flag is completed that gives the date and possibly the number of books that were read to earn the squares.

The completed flag makes a fantastic background for group photographs. Be sure to notify the media when the flag is completed to publicize your school's emphasis on reading.

Star pattern:

Flag design:

Blue with white stars	Red squares
	White squares
Blue with white stars	Red squares
Blue with white stars	White squares
	Red squares
Blue with white stars	White squares
	Red squares
White squares	
Red squares	
White squares	
Red squares	
White squares	
Red squares	

If a school-wide flag wall chart is not being used, a flag done in a slightly different way would work well for a classroom. Make the flag with the red and white stripes and a field of blue. Using a dark marker or tape, divide the flag up into ten areas which can represent points or percentages. Use a white star as the child's marker. The star would move along until 100 percent had been accomplished and then the star would be placed on the blue field. A new star could be given to the child to begin the process again.

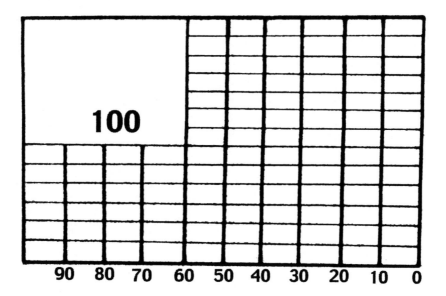

For another type of individual classroom wall chart, start with an outline map of the continental United States. This can be a large commercially produced map or one made on any kind of large piece of paper. Heavy brown contractor's paper, which is inexpensive, holds up well for a year's worth of charting reading progress. Use an opaque projector to enlarge the outline map to the desired size.

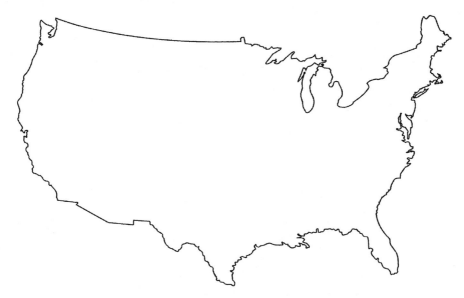

There are so many possibilities—from covered wagons to race cars to a specific period of time in America's history—to use as the subject of the wall chart. Choose something that has a special meaning for your school or hometown.

Creating the wall chart might become a classroom project. After choosing the theme relating to the U.S., the students could paint the background. The map could have the rivers painted in, along with mountains, deserts, and other features and your particular state highlighted.

Divide the map into sections which represent points or percentages as dictated by your reading program. These lines can be drawn in with a dark marker or done with colored plastic tape or masking tape. Use your computer to print the marking designations for each section. The more "professional" the display looks, the more authentic it will look to the students and will be taken more seriously.

Some great ideas for markers for your display are tennis shoes, cars or trucks, footprints, covered wagons, your school's mascot, or suitcases.

It is a good idea to laminate the marker pieces, as they need to last for the year and hopefully they will be moving daily.

What will your plan be for the student who quickly moves across the map? One possibility is to have a designated parking area marked "job well done!" The marker is put there and the child receives a new one to begin again. For some students it becomes a matter of personal pride to see how many markers they can move across the chart in the year's time.

Take a good look at your Social Studies curriculum. Can this chart be coordinated with your course of study? Tying the chart to the regular curriculum gives it more validity and they both complement each other nicely.

One idea might be to move from east to west on the map chart and tie these states to the seasons. This allows you to begin in New England in September and October when the leaves will be changing color. Plan a coordinating activity to feature this area and the beautiful foliage. It could be winter across the Plains states or into the Rocky Mountain area by the time your readers have progressed across the chart. Finish the year along the Pacific coast with a beach party.

A pattern for an outline map and some possible chart marker patterns are provided.

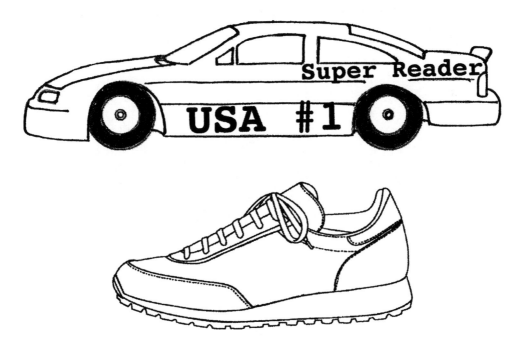

Special Events

Plan at least one big library sponsored event for each grade for the year. This sounds like a lot of work but don't try to do everything yourself. Collab-

orate with the classroom teachers and try to tie the event to a unit of study.
Here are some ideas .

A. The World Series.

Who doesn't like baseball? Put up a large U.S. map and mark the
hometown cities of American and National League teams with little
red and blue flags. Pull out all those baseball biographies and baseball
fiction stories for a display. Hang some photographs of famous players,
past and present. Using comic book–style balloons, add words as
though the picture could talk. Center all the words around reading.
"I'd rather be reading."
"Reading really turns me on!"
"I'm positive that I turned in that library book."
"The book said to hold the bat just like this."
Position some bases around the room with home plate at the
checkout desk.

Ask the P.E. teacher to help you organize a student-faculty baseball game on a Friday afternoon. This would probably be best done
with your oldest students. Encourage those special teachers (art,
music, special education, the counselor, gifted teacher, reading, even
the principal) to participate.

B. Celebrate your state's birthday.

Have a school-wide celebration inviting in your state representa-
tive and state senator. Send an invitation to your town's mayor and
even the governor. Invite everyone you can think of who holds an
elected office. They are generally happy to come, especially in an
election year. Have them explain to the children what they do in
their elected position.

Create a list of all the famous Americans from your state. *The
World Almanac* lists those with the state's current information. Display photographs and books about these people. Encourage your students to come dressed as one of these famous people to assume their
identity for the day. Provide a name tag for every student so that
even though they might not have come dressed in costume, they can
still participate. Ask a trivia question each day that could be
answered about one of these famous people.

Host a movie-fest for the day of any videos on your state that you can find. This might include historical items, conservation topics, your state government, or a short movie based on a fiction book that takes place in your state.

Proudly display your state's symbols. Encourage your art teacher to help you provide art activities with these symbols.

C. Career Day.

Work with your school counselor to sponsor a career day.

Invite people with all types of occupations to talk to the children. Put up signs that say "Future Famous Americans Here!" Give each child a name tag that says

Future Famous_____. They fill in the blank with doctor, nurse, policeman, etc.

Display books on all types of careers. Use a variety of hats in your display, including a fireman's helmet, a military hat, a baseball cap, an old straw hat, a top hat, any sort of hat worn for a particular job.

D. Election Time.

Early November is a great chance to pull out those books on voting, citizenship, the political parties, and even the book *So You Want to Be President.* This is not an opportunity to push your particular political agenda but to inform your students on the political process and their civic responsibilities.

Sponsor a mock election in your school and offer to set up voting booths in your library. Coordinate this with the classroom teachers. Decorating can be as simple as red, white, and blue crepe paper plus stars and balloons. Usually a week or two is long enough for this type of display.

E. Cowboy Day.

Use the theme "Rope 'em and Read 'em! and encourage the children to come dressed in their cowboy finery with the exception of guns. Start the day with an assembly. Perhaps you have some high school age students who can rope or even participate in rodeos. Ask them to put on an exhibition for your students.

Ask some of your faculty to star in a melodrama for the event. This is a great way to get some audience participation and the children will love to see their teachers in these new roles. Write your own or try this one.

Cowboy Melodrama

Characters:	Narrator
	Badley Bookswiper
	Ima Reader
	Little Betty Booklover
	Sheriff Coach
	a person to hold the "BOO" sign and the "HURRAY" sign
	Props needed: a cart of library books
	a chair
	a sheriff's star and cowboy hat for the coach
	a black cape for the villain
	sign saying "BOO" and one saying "HURRAY"
Notes:	The narrator does all the talking and is the only one who will need a microphone. The actors merely pantomime their parts with exaggerated reactions in all the scenes. The sheriff is played by the coach because the coach is usually a very popular faculty member that the children don't often associate with reading.
	Ask the audience to "BOO" for the villain whenever they see the sign and *only* when they see the sign. The same instructions go for the "HURRAY" sign.
Narrator:	One day as Little Betty Booklover was sitting reading her favorite library book, out of nowhere popped Badley Bookswiper. ["BOO"][He is wearing a black cape and acting very much the villain.] Badley grabbed her book and ran off down the street. [Badley runs out of the area with the book under his arm.] Little Betty Booklover was so sad and she began to cry and cry. [Betty should stand up and pretend to cry and be very distraught.] It was her favorite library book that was taken and how would she explain to the librarian that it was stolen?
	Not long after Badley's evil deed, we find Ima Reader pushing a cart of library books down the hall toward the library.

While she pushed the cart, Ima read her favorite book. Out popped Badley Bookswiper once again, but, instead of taking just one book, he took the whole cart of library books, including Ima Reader's favorite book, and ran down the hallway. ["BOO"] [Badley pushes the cart quickly off the stage area.] What just happened? What should she do? How was she going to finish her book report? Oh my, my, my!!

Ima Reader and Little Betty Booklover went to see Sheriff Coach. Surely he could help them. "Please help us find our library books, Sheriff Coach."

Since Sheriff Coach could do anything, he started his search for Badley Bookswiper. He looked everywhere. [Sheriff pretends to look in totally ridiculous areas like the trash can, etc.]

Finally Sheriff Coach captures Badley Bookswiper and brings him and the cart of library books back to the girls. ["HURRAY"] Sheriff Coach says, "Badley Bookswiper took your books because he wanted to learn to read. You looked so happy with your books that he wanted to read, too. It just looked like so much fun. He's really sorry for what he did. [Badley needs to look really pitiful and remorseful.] Do you girls think you could help Badley learn to read and to learn to use the library?"

Ima Reader and Little Betty Booklover were thrilled to get their favorite library books back and agreed to help Badley Bookswiper become a reader, too. They all head off to the library. [They go off stage pushing the cart of books and chatting happily together. Ima Reader puts her arm around Badley's shoulder.]

Sheriff Coach smiles, puffs up his chest, and says "I'm *so* good! Now I can get back to *my* library book!"
["HURRAY"]
The End.

Hang up some photographs of old cowboy movie stars. In the old movies the good guys always wear white hats. This could lead into a discussion of good vs. bad and what it means to be ethical.

Display all those books the children love on horses, Jesse James, Calamity Jane, Wyatt Earp, Doc Holliday, etc. Use brands around the room or just draw some on a piece of paper to serve as the base for your book display.

Possibly the P.E. teacher would have the students play horseshoes on this day or even square dance. And ... how about hotdogs and beans for lunch?

F. Frontier and Pioneer Days.

Get out those *Little House on the Prairie* books along with all those great biographies on Daniel Boone, Lewis and Clark, and all those great pioneers, plus books on the Pony Express and the Oregon and Santa Fe trails.

Encourage the children to come dressed for the day in pioneer costumes. For a special treat, feature a type of game that would have been played during that period in our nation's history. If possible, cook over a fire as they did back then. *The Little House Cookbook* could help with some ideas for cooking.

The Oregon Trail computer software would fit perfectly in this celebration.

G. The '50s.

Use the theme "Read and Rock and Roll" and decorate the library for the '50s. Elvis Presley's birthday (or death date) would be a great time for a celebration. Playing rock and roll music before school would be attention-getting and fun.

Use a refrigerator box to create a simple juke box and don't forget to add some lights. Most of your students won't recognize what a record is but hang some or use some 7" laminated circles of black construction paper from the ceiling. Put up lots of music notes also.

Sponsor a sock hop on a Friday afternoon in the school gym. Having it for a short time during the school day will allow everyone the opportunity to attend. Encourage the students to dress up for the day in their poodle skirts, white T-shirts, rolled up jeans, and penny loafers. Have a hula-hooping contest.

Get out your school's yearbooks from the '50s. The students will be amazed at what school activities looked like back then. Reading rocks!

H. Beach Party.

February is "Blah-Buster" month. Beat the blahs by hosting a school-wide beach day. Swimming suits would be out but shorts, Hawaiian shirts, sunglasses, leis, beach towels, and flipflops are the "in" thing for the day. Play Beach Boy' music over the intercom system before school starts to set the mood for the day. Ask the P.E. teacher to play beach ball volleyball with the classes.

Set up beach chairs and lawn chairs in the library along with a beach umbrella to create a great quiet reading area. Feature books on scuba diving, surfing, sharks, and all kinds of cool underwater creatures. Use sea shells around the room for a little extra pizazz.

I. The 100th Day of School.

Encourage each class to read 100 books during the day. If each child reads four or five easy fiction books, it can be done. Start the day with 100 balloons blown up and taped to the wall. Each time a child reads a book, he is permitted to pop a balloon.

Set aside 100 minutes of free-time reading during the day.

J. Dr. Seuss' Birthday—March 2.

Host a Dr. Seuss Read-a-thon. Try to read out loud every Dr. Seuss book in the library on that day. For each book read during the day, give the students a strip of white or red construction paper. Construct a red and white striped paper chain. Attempt to make a chain that reaches the length of the longest hallway.

Host a silly hat day. Encourage the students to create really silly hats to wear on that day. Offer simple, inexpensive prizes. Depending on the size of your school, ask your teachers or parents' group to bring in cupcakes or cookies for the event.

K. County Fair Games.

As a reward for your readers, host a game time. Enlist the help of your fellow teachers. Keep the games simple with an old time fair atmosphere or farm theme with the emphasis on the fun of playing and not on winning or losing. Give everyone prizes such as pencils, fast food coupons, gum, or candy.

Some games to consider are duck pond, fishing hole, bowling, cupcake or cookie walk, Nerf basketball, plastic egg toss, wet sponge toss, dunking booth, hockey, horseshoes, feed the pigs, ring toss, Golf, water balloons, hula hoop toss, and face painting.

Around the World

There are so many places to visit and so little time. An entire school year's decorating could be built around our world with its awesome cultures and fabulous scenery. Coordinate with your art and music teachers to organize a theme that crosses many curriculums.

Begin the year with a grand welcome. The word "hello" in many different languages would be a good start. Cut the letters from construction paper and glue them to strips of bright poster paper. Be sure to include the name of the country in which the language is spoken.

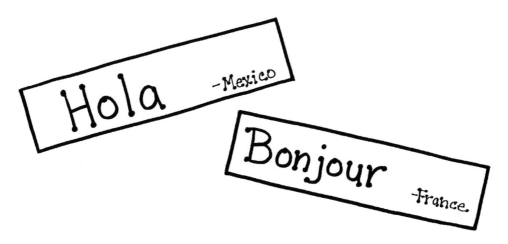

Here is the word equivalent for "hello" in some different languages:

Danish	Goodag
Dutch	Goede dag, Hallo

Finnish	Hei
German	Guten Tag
Hawaiian	Aloha
Armenian	Barev
Irish	Dia duit
Italian	Ciao
Swahili	Jambo
Portuguese	Olà
Japanese	Konnichi wa
Norwegian	Hallo
Polish	Dzien' dobry
Hebrew	Shalom
French	Bonjour
Spanish	Hola
Mandarin Chinese	Ny hao
Swedish	Hej

Check the Internet if you are looking for a particular language that is not listed here.

Follow this same concept at Christmas time with "Merry Christmas" in different languages. Create simple paper banners with cut paper letters decorated with ribbons and foil trim.

Portuguese	Boas Festas
Bulgarian	Tchestita Koleda
Mandarin Chinese	Kung His Hsin Nien bing Chu Shen Tan
Danish	Glaedelig Jul
Finnish	Hyvaa joulua
French	Joyeux Noel
German	Froehliche Weihnachten
Greek	Kala Christouyenna!
Hawaiian	Mele Kalikimaka
Icelandic	Gleileg Jol
Indonesian	Selamat Hari Natal
Norwegian	God Jul
Spanish	Feliz Navidad
Thai	Sawadee Pee Mai

Go online and research your favorite country to see how their language gives this greeting.

Hang up flags from other countries. These can be made from poster paper. *The World Almanac* is a great source of flags of the world. It is possible to find relatively easy ones to make. Include a label with the country's name. This is something that your older students could do for the library or might be done in art class.

Display a large world map with the caption "Where in the world have you been?" Dig in that pile of old maps that you've been saving and get them out

for your students to look at. How about dragging out some of those old *National Geographic* magazines that you've got tons of for the children to look at in the reading area?

Provide your principal with interesting facts about the world to read each morning at announcement time. These facts are available online or look through some of your atlases, almanacs, and other reference books. If the announcement idea doesn't work for your school, just print a fact and post it each day. Every day with this theme is a teaching opportunity.

Make a word search or word puzzle for each continent. Go to www.puzzle maker.com to make puzzles that will really appeal to your students and be educational at the same time.

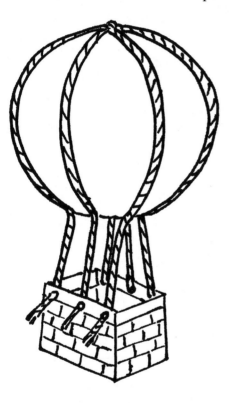

Your trip around the world might be by hot air balloon. An easy way to make a hot air balloon for your display is to use a beach ball.

Cut three very long pieces of string all the same length. Tie them all together in the middle in one knot. Tape the string to the top of the beach ball with the knot in the center and the six string pieces evenly spaced around the beach ball. Be sure that there is plenty of string to reach around the balloon and still have enough to attach a basket. Pull the string down the sides of the ball and tape each string in place. Tie on the basket.

A small brown lunch sack cut off about a fourth of the way down works great for a basket. Fold down the top to make it a little stronger. Punch three holes on each side to attach the string. Use a marker and draw in some lines to resemble a basket weave pattern.

Put a small version of your school mascot in the basket holding a map or even a paper book.

Look through your aircraft books and consider a vintage airplane complete with your school's mascot as the symbol for this around the world theme. Tie all the decorating to your school's reading program. Use your little mascot in the plane everywhere—bookmarks, T-shirt designs, etc.

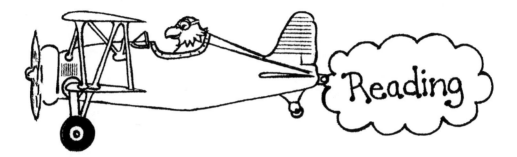

Put the airplane in motion as part of a hanging display.

To make this, cut two large circles the same size from red posterboard. Attach them to either side of a styrofoam wreath using straight pins. The styrofoam gives the circles some dimension and makes your display 3-D.

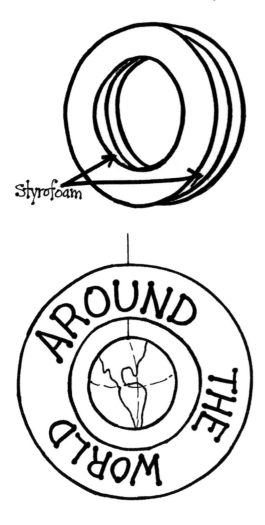

Hang a small inflatable globe with fishing line in the center of the circles. It needs to be small enough to fit in the space and still be able to turn independently.

Cut out the letters for "Around the World" out of black construction paper and glue them around the circle.

Make a copy of the airplane with your school's mascot, color it, and laminate it. Attach the plane to a piece of black wire. Bend the wire and push one end into the styrofoam along the outside of the circle. Bend the wire to position the plane so it looks like it is flying around the world.

To create a reading display that charts the school's reading progress for a program such as Reading Counts or Accelerated Reader, use 4" squares of construction paper in varying colors. Each time a student earns 10 points, have them put their name and the date on one of the squares. Begin putting up the squares horizontally near where the wall meets the ceiling. Position the airplane as though it is leaving a smoke screen trail of colorful squares behind. Move the airplane each time you add more squares.

It is very effective if a different color square is used for each grade. It's very easy to spot which grade is doing the most reading. When a child reaches her reading goal, have her add a "fireball" to the airplane's trail. This is a piece of yellow paper and red paper made to look like an explosion. She adds her name and the date she received it.

Challenge your students to move the airplane around the entire school by reading. Provide a drop-off container in the library for the squares.

Feature a different continent each month, including books on the countries located there, the languages involved, folk tales, art, sports, food—the possibilities are endless. Using www.puzzlemaker.com, create word search puzzles for each continent to have at the checkout desk for those students who complete assignments early or to grab on their way out of the library.

Asia

Try this style letter pattern for the letters of your display. Use a shiny gold paper for the letters to give a more elegant effect.

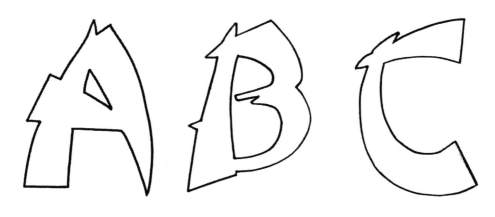

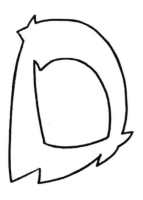

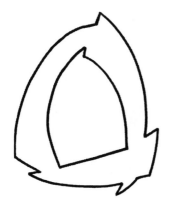

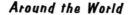

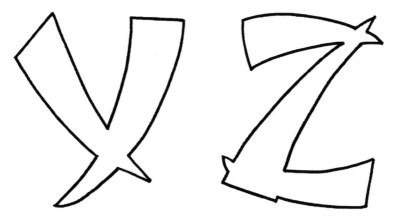

Along with maps of Asia lying out for the children to see, hang Japanese lanterns and consider some Japanese kites. These are easy and can be very beautiful. Start with a large rectangular piece of heavy paper. Fold the paper in half lengthwise. With the fold on the top, draw half of a fish.

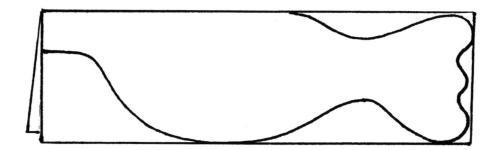

Cut out the fish shape, being very careful not to cut off the fold. Draw in the fish's details and color them with crayons or markers on both sides of the fold. Red is a very important color in Asian countries so feature it prominently. Open up the fish. Fold

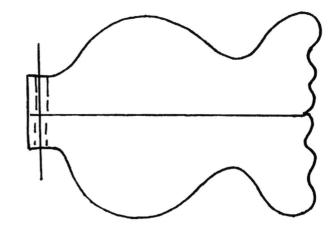

the mouth area toward the inside two times with a piece of thin wire approximately 12" long in the fold. This helps to strengthen the mouth and allows the mouth to form an "O" shape which helps to semi-inflate the fish.

Fold the fish and twist the wire together to form the mouth. Staple the fish together along the bottom and along the top open area. Leave the tail end open. Add some foil details and long pieces of shiny ribbon or crepe paper. Slide the fish onto a piece of bamboo, a dowel rod, or an old broom handle and then hang with fishing line. Position several of these beautiful and graceful fish around your library. Use straight pins to fasten the ends of the ribbon to the ceiling tiles to give the illusion that the fish is flying in the breeze.

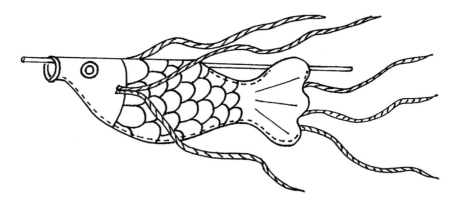

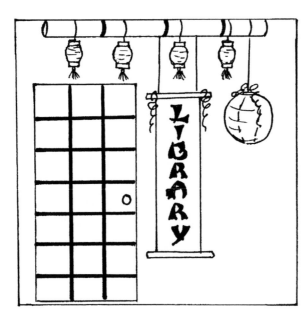

For an interesting door decoration, take a large sheet of white paper which is the same size as the door. Using some watery black tempra paint, create a very simple painting of a house and tree. Look at an example of traditional Japanese art.

When the painting is dry, cover the entire painting with wax paper. Use black electrical tape to hold everything together by creating a window pane pattern. When finished, this will resemble the paper wall of a Japanese house.

A carpet tube painted red with a touch of gold looks good hung from fishing line over the door. Use black electrical tape around the tube in approximately three stripes. Hang some colorful lanterns from this tube.

Additional panels can be created by hanging strips of paper on a piece of bamboo or a dowel rod. Make it in the same way by painting and then covering the paper with wax paper. Finish up with the black tape. Thin gold ribbon can be tied on for more color and sparkle.

Make hanging banners on strips of red paper with gold letters that say "Fiction" and "Nonfiction," or make similar banners for any special book displays.

South America

We usually think of the rain forest when we think of South America. This is a colorful way to add some pizazz to a book display. Cover the table for the display with some brightly colored fabric. Make a palm tree to stand next to the table from a carpet tube.

Carpet tubes are generally free at lumberyards or flooring stores. Use a hand saw to cut the tube to your desired length. To keep your palm tree standing straight and tall, build a base out of scrap lumber. Three small boards are required for the base. Nail two boards together to create an X shape. The third smaller board is nailed so that it stands up in the center of the X. It may be necessary to add a small board on the bottom edge of each end of the top board of the X to create better balance.

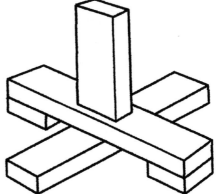

Set the tube down onto the vertical board and use a few screws to secure it in place. Wrap the tube in strips of brown paper cut in a fringed pattern. The bases are not really very attractive so make plans to cover them with tan fabric or brown paper.

Old wire coat hangers will give your palm leaves their stem.

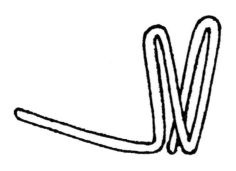

Using pliers, close the sharp end of the wire into a circle so that no one will accidently walk into it and be cut. Bend the wire end to resemble the illustration.

Use green poster paper for the palm leaves. Make a pattern out of a piece of newspaper. Start with an elongated football shape, using a zigzag pattern to finish up the leaf design.

Tape the paper onto the wire stem you have made. To attach the finished leaf, just slide the wire onto the top of the tube.

Each palm tree needs at least five leaves. The wire stem will allow you to bend the leaves and create a pleasing arrangement.

To add more color to the display, make some tissue paper flowers. These can be made by using three sheets of tissue paper, any size. Choose attention-getting colors of tissue paper. Stack the three sheets on top of each other and fold the papers back and forth accordion style. Continue this process all the way across the paper.

Use a twist-tie or piece of wire around the center of the folded paper. Slowly begin to pull up the first sheet of paper carefully toward the twist-tie. Do this to the top sheet on both sides of the center. Pulling both of these to the center will allow you to form a circle. If you pull up all the paper on one side and then do the other side, your flower will look more like a bow tie. Repeat the process until all the layers of paper have been pulled up and form a flower.

Thin green ribbon or rolls of paper ribbon serve well as vines. Just twist-tie on the flowers along with a few tissue paper leaves hot glued on. Drape these around your display area to tie everything together.

Display books about butterflies, tree frogs, chocolate, the Incans, the Galapagos Islands, South American countries, and the rain forest, and display greetings in each language.

Europe

Wow, what fabulous tourist sites to visit! Feature the Eiffel Tower, Stonehenge, castles, the Leaning Tower of Pisa, battles of World War II, Olympic books, French or Italian cooking, kings and queens; oh, so many things to share! You could have fun with just the fairy tales, or a European Christmas.

Use maps for the background of your bulletin board and consider displaying the books in an open suitcase. Use photographs of well known European sites. Omit the name of the spot and put a question mark. Your students will enjoy testing their knowledge. The majority of flags of this region are easy to make. Hang the flags around the room with some greeting in each language.

Antarctica

This is a great continent to feature during the winter months. It is a great chance to use some snowflakes, snowmen, sleds, and penguins. Let's face it, there just aren't too many established places for us to visit in Antarctica, so, just celebrate snow.

Cut lots of snowflakes and staple them together to create a snowflake chain. Cover the table with a dark tablecloth with a white smaller tablecloth over that. Add some glittered snowflakes to shine as accent pieces.

There are many ways to make snowmen. Use a piece of scrap carpet

tube. A small child's stocking cap or even an old knitted sock pulled over the top of the tube serves as the hat. Make an orange construction paper cone for the nose or use a real carrot. Just cut a small hole in the tube and hot glue it in place. Using a real carrot would be a temporary nose! Black construction paper circles work for eyes and the mouth. Add two small sticks for arms. Wrap a scarf around the base.

Using a white lunch bag is another great way to make a snowman. Add a nose made from a cone of orange construction paper. Add small circles for the eyes and mouth. Glue on a hat cut from a piece of construction paper.

Australia

Australia is the largest island and the smallest continent. Use a round table and create an island of your own. Feature books about the many deserts there, the Tasmanian devil, the Sydney Opera House, and, of course, boomerangs. Students are always fascinated by this continent so use the opportunity to talk about the difference in our seasons and theirs.

An assembly possibility

Many times you need an assembly idea to jump start a year of reading. Ask your teachers to participate in "The Amazing Race." Have all the teachers in a grade work together as a team for the big race while the students cheer them on. The teams are timed, with the quickest time being awarded first place. A stop watch and time keeper will be needed for each team competing.

This race course should be set up in a gym or large area of the playground. Set up at least three separate courses to speed up the process. The teachers on the team work to complete an activity for each continent. They can be done in any order. The teachers must complete the activity and move on to the next one as quickly as possible. The stop watch starts when they begin the first event and stops after all have been completed.

Europe: The Tour de France is done on a tricycle or scooter. Set up some orange cones or chairs in a large figure eight pattern. Each teacher on the team must ride the tricycle or scooter in the figure eight as quickly as possible.

Australia "Down Under" Have a tarp on the ground with a box or bucket of dirt complete with real worms. The teachers must dig in the dirt and pull out at least ten worms. Have the time keeper there to verify the ten worms. Provide hand wipes so they can clean up their hands.

Africa: Using a roll of toilet paper, the teachers must wrap one of their team members as a mummy using the entire roll of toilet paper.

South America: Soccer is the big sport! Using their feet, the teachers must pass the ball the length of the gym and back and kick it into the goal.

North America: One of the teachers must rope a "cow" (chair). The remaining teachers must brand the "cow" with a Post-it note that lists their grade and all the teachers' initials on the team.

Asia: Fill a small bucket with packing peanuts. The teachers working together must use chopsticks to move all the packing peanuts from the bucket to another container.

Antarctica: Freeze solid a small paper cup of water. You will need one for each team. The teachers must work together to thaw this ice cube. They may not put it in their mouth or break it up, but must rub it on their clothes, in their hands, etc. Every bit must be gone!

This sounds like a lot but the race will go very quickly. It would be a good idea to explain the race in detail to all the participants prior to the assembly. In the rush to begin, you might overlook an important instruction.

Here is a list of materials needed for this assembly idea.

- a stop watch for each course area

- a person to time each course area

- one roll of toilet paper per team

- orange cones or two chairs for the Tour de France figure eight

- a tricycle or scooter for each course area

- a bucket of packing peanuts and another empty container for each course area

- a set of chopsticks for each teacher for each course area

- a rope and chair for lassoing a "cow" for each course area

- Post-it notes and markers for each course area

- a large ice cube for each team

- two tarps for each course area (for Australia and Antarctica)

- a soccer ball and goal for each course area

- a bucket of worms (15–20) for each course area

- hand wipes for the Australia area in each course

- some type of prize for the team with the fastest time. Thirty minutes of time away from their class is a great prize and there is no expense involved. Someone, such as the principal, must volunteer to take the class.

Give Yourself a Gift

This idea works well for the Christmas holidays or for any time of the year. The only difference is the color scheme you choose and a few decorating choices. The words for the display are "Give yourself a gift. Read a good book!"

Ask your faculty and staff to fill out a very simple questionnaire. Ask them what their all-time favorite book is. This could be a book from any time in their life and it isn't necessary for this book to be in your library.

One of the great parts of this theme is that the students often find that they have something in common with a teacher—the same favorite book. Other times it has been an encouragement for a student to search out a particular book just because Mr._____ or Mrs._____ said it was their favorite. Put as many of the books as possible on display.

The display itself is easy. Make a simple box drawing and photocopy one on several different colors of construction paper or card stock. Use a black marker and neatly write in one of the favorite book titles from your survey. Add ribbon and a bow. Make a gift card and attach it to the bow.

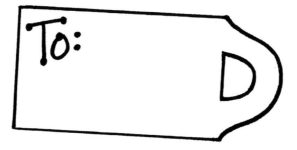

You probably should make two different box patterns to give the display a little variety. A view from each side of the box will make the whole look more interesting.

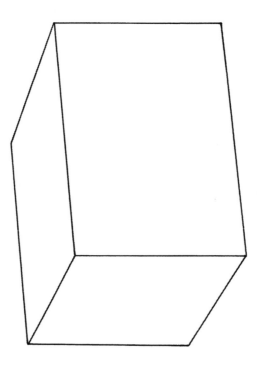

The beauty of using this idea for a time other than Christmas is that it can stay up indefinitely. Forget red and green as the ribbon colors and use every color. Everyone will enjoy that this display was personally designed for your school.

A Paint Theme

Paint cans are cool! Empty or full, they provide so many decorating opportunities. Build a room-wide display centered around the art of painting and painting materials. Add a phrase like: "Reading adds color to your life!"

To create a giant paintbrush, use a long carpet tube. Wrap the tube in brown mailing paper. Wrap one end in black paper to give the handle of your brush a nice finished end. Using silver posterboard, create a cone shape that will fit on the other end of the carpet tube.

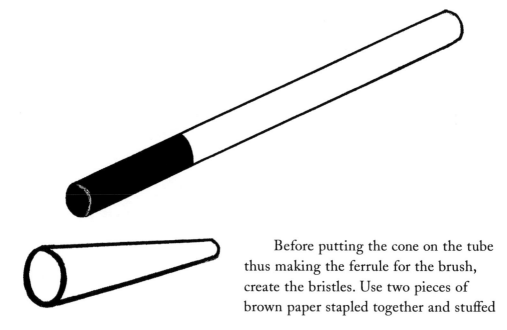

Before putting the cone on the tube thus making the ferrule for the brush, create the bristles. Use two pieces of brown paper stapled together and stuffed with small pieces of newspaper. Tape it into the inside of the ferrule. Use a black marker to draw on the hairs of the brush.

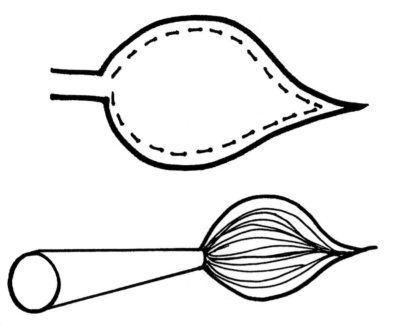

Slide the ferrule on to the tube and glue it in place. Use heavy weight fishing line to hang this paintbrush from the ceiling or set the brush on the top of a bookshelf.

You might pretend that you have been painting with this brush by painting the bristle area about halfway up from the tip of the bristles. Create a drip of the same color to use and label the drip for a type of books such as biographies.

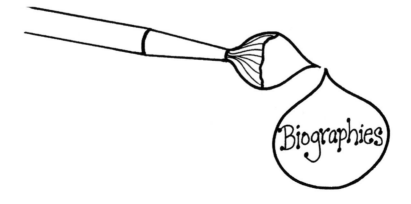

Use cast off paint cans by creating new labels. These might be Dewey decimal areas or just mystery blue, fantasy purple, or even orange adventure stories, or use the cans as bookends. It is possible to purchase new empty paint cans to use as holders for shelf markers, pencils, rulers, and other items.

A paint ladder works well to hold new books. Just set the books on the ladder rungs and even set a small table under the ladder with a drop cloth for the tablecloth. The students can use paint stir sticks for shelf markers. Ask at your paint store for a donation of sticks.

A Medieval Theme

Dragons, castles, knights, lords and ladies are exciting to children and are a great reading motivator. Use a theme slogan like: "We're all fired up for reading!" or "Joust Read!"

Large crowns made from posterboard put around hula hoops look great hanging from the ceiling.

Start with a strip of posterboard that will reach around the hula hoop. The width of the strip is determined by how tall you would like your crown to be. Fold up the bottom edge of the strip until the folded area is approximately 6" wide. Clip the bottom edge to within ½" of the fold.

Position the hula hoop inside the fold and bend the posterboard around to com-

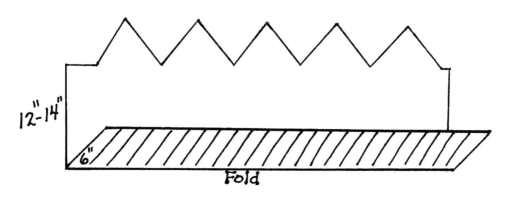

plete the circle. Tape the cut slits to the crown on the inside as you are form-ing the circle. Staple the circle together.

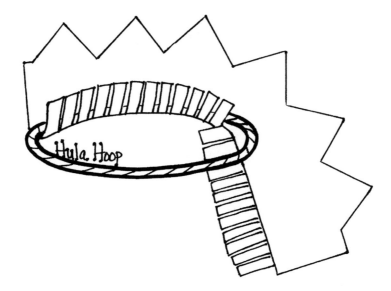

Cut a thin strip of posterboard and glue it to the inside of the crown to cover the tape. Spray the entire crown with gold spray paint. Cut shiny foil paper in geometric shapes for jewels. Other trims can be hot glued on. Hang the crown from the ceiling with fishing line.

Cover old office chairs with simple slip covers. Discount stores often have inexpensive doubleknit fabric that can be used to stitch up a quick "royal" chair cover up. These can become thrones and the area they sit in might be referred to as "The Throne Room." You might speak of this area in a low whisper as though it is for royalty. Add a few satin covered pil-lows. The children love the extravagance of them and will be careful in their use.

Create banners to highlight the different areas of the library. These can be made from poster paper or posterboard. They are quick to make and look great hung from the ceiling. Cut long strips of paper and hang as though it is ribbon. Choose a color scheme such as blue, green, and purple, or red, blue and purple. Add some glitz with gold or silver trim or inexpensive rib-bon.

Do you have a gazing ball in your yard? If so, why not use it in a display in your library? It will look great with a group of fairy tale books.

Create arched doorways out of white paper or brown mailing paper. Measure the doorway and then make a pattern out of newspaper. Outline the stones in permanent black marker. Using a sponge, dab on some gray paint, a light shade of brown, a little white, and splatter with some black so that it resembles stone. Individual stones can be made also.

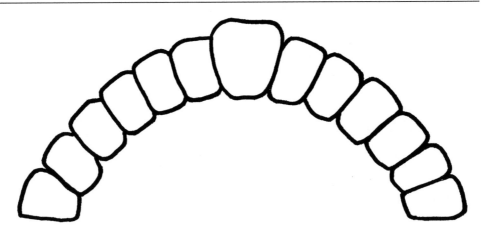

Creating arched windows will help to continue the theme. Use heavy brown paper cut to cover the width of your window sections. Create the stone pattern similar to the door arches. If you have single windows, just make an arch like you do for your door. If the windows are long and thin, add strips of paper on either side of the arch to help anchor the arch in place. Add some pennants on either side to add some color and glitz.

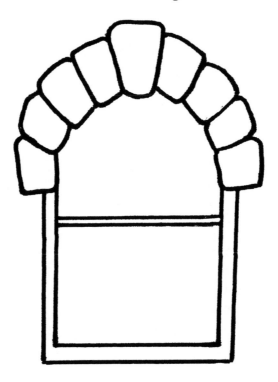

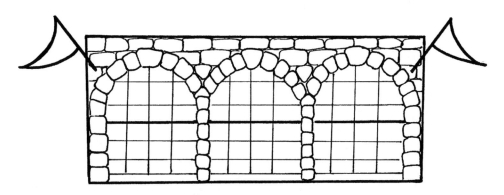

If you are really daring, use the opaque projector to help you make a suit of armor. Brown mailing paper is very strong and can take paint quite well. Outline the suit of armor in black permanent marker and then paint with silver paint. Put some bookcovers, a magazine, or a newspaper under one of the arms. Add a banner on a paper pole with the word "READ."

For a count of your check-out, create a simple door chart from brown paper. Find a clip art knight on a horse. Copy it, color it, and laminate it to move up the road toward the castle each time another 1,000 books are checked out. Use a light colored marker to color in the blocks as that number of books has been checked out.

Cover your library door

with brown mailing paper. Using a black marker, draw in a few lines to help it look as though your door is made of big old boards. Use black construction paper for the hinges. Add some individual stones around the door and a stone archway over the door. Position your suit of armor next to the door as though it is guarding the library.

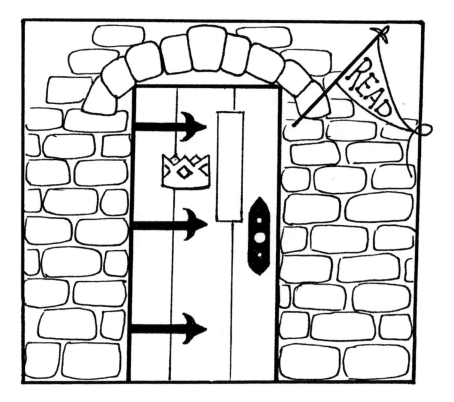

The Gigantic Garden

The time period in January that seems rather dead after all the hoopla of the holidays is a great time to try creating a gigantic garden. This provides you with an alternative to the traditional snowflakes and really surprises the children. Approach this from a worm's point of view with each item made to look "king size" or like something out of *Alice's Adventures in Wonderland*.

Flowers

Start with some large flowers that go floor to ceiling. For the flower stem, use a carpet tube on a stand as described in the "Around the World" chapter. Paint the tube green or wrap it in green paper. Green wrapping paper works well when cut in strips and wrapped around the tube. Hot glue the ends to hold the paper in place. Cut a few simple leaves out of posterboard and hot glue or staple them on.

For the flower, cut petals from heavy posterboard. Red or orange petals look great. Use a circle of foam insulation or styrofoam for the center of the flower. Cover the foam with paper, preferably yellow. Attach the petals to the center with straight pins and hot glue.

To strengthen the petals, hot glue a small piece of bamboo, a thin stick, or a strip of heavy cardboard that has been painted the color of your petals to the backside. Hot glue the whole flower to the stem. Use a staple gun to attach it in a few spots for a little added protection.

Using a paper punch, make a hole in at least two of the top petals String fishing line in the hole and, using a ceiling clip or a paper clip, hook this to the ceiling. It will help to keep the flower steady.

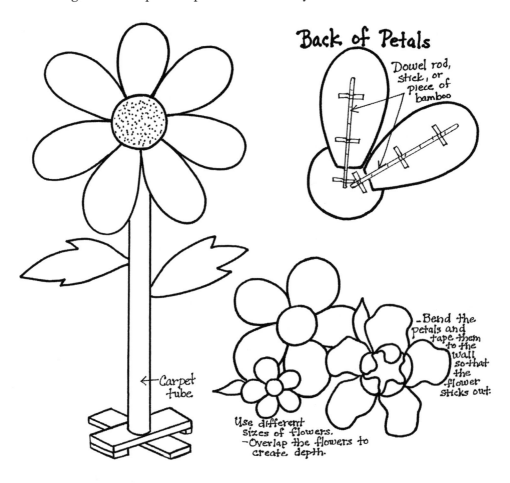

Make really large paper flowers from posterboard or poster paper. When you attach them to the wall, do so in a way that makes them appear more 3D. For some of your flowers, bend the petals in different ways so that all of the flower is not plastered against the wall. You should try to create a little depth by having some flat against the wall in the back and some sticking out in the front. Vary the size of the flowers to create more interest and add a few leaves tucked in here and there.

Mushroom

Another eye catching display item is a mushroom. This is a more advanced project but one that can be done if you take your time.

Start with an umbrella you are willing to sacrifice. Open the umbrella and cover the top with some batting. This is the material that is put inside a quilt. Using a needle and thread, tack the batting to the umbrella on the underside. Using a piece of doubleknit or other stretchy fabric in a color you like, stretch the fabric over the batting and sew it to the underside of the umbrella.

Hand stitch fabric to umbrella.

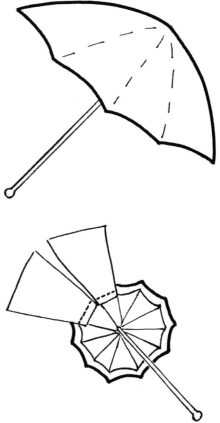

Cut some felt circles of different sizes and glue them on the top of the fabric. Felt that is peel and stick works well.

For the underneath part of the mushroom, you will need some light tan, off white, or light gray fabric. Cut the fabric into large pieces. Hand stitch a piece of fabric onto the underside. When you fold this piece to the inside later, your stitches will be covered. You will need to do this with strips until you make it completely around the umbrella. Fold the strips toward the center, making sure that the entire area is covered. Use a rubber band to gather and secure the fabric around the umbrella handle.

For the mushroom stem, cut a piece of carpet tube that is at least as long as the umbrella handle. Use a plastic gallon ice cream container and cut a hole in the lid so that the carpet tube can slide through and stand upright. Put a few rocks into the tube to give the bottom more weight.

Using more batting, wrap the tube and ice cream container. Stitch it to itself or hot glue it to the tube. Cover this with a piece of stretchy fabric in a color that looks nice with the color of the mushroom top.

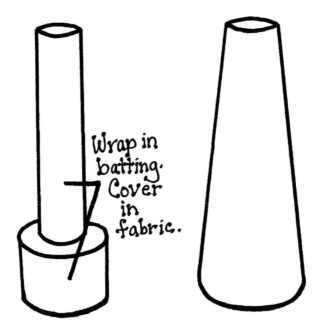

Wrap in batting. Cover in fabric.

Set the umbrella handle down inside the carpet tube and you now have an awesome mushroom. Set the mushroom up on a bookshelf. Do not be surprised if the underside begins to sag a little as time goes by. It actually make the mushroom look even better. Position an animal or critter reading a book leaning against your new mushroom.

Butterfly

Some really big butterflies would look nice hanging from the ceiling. To make one you will need a wrapping paper cardboard tube, a styrofoam ball (the size depends on the size of the butterfly you want to make), black duct tape, some heavy wire, two long black pipe cleaners and a large sheet of poster paper—enough to cut four wings.

93

Tape the styrofoam ball to the cardboard tube with the black duct tape. Insert two pipe cleaners into the styrofoam ball and curl them for antennae.

Form the wing shape you want from the heavy wire. Create a newspaper pattern by tracing the wire shape and adding two or three inches around the wire. Cut four of these from your poster paper.

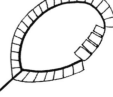

Cut slits around the paper and carefully hot glue the paper over the wire. Work your way around the wire shape. Do this for all four wing pieces. You might consider making the two top sections one size and the two bottom ones much larger. Use a marker to draw lines on the wing. Foil paper and other items like large sequins can be glued on to decorate the wings.

Twist a set of wings together and then use black duct tape to attach the wings to the tube.

Hang the butterfly with fishing line.

Caterpillar

For a temporary caterpillar, use balloons. Blow up balloons and tape them in a caterpillar formation for a fun part of your display. Replace balloons as needed.

Bumblebee

Make some cool bumblebees to go with these phrases: "Bee a reader!" "Reading is the BUZZ word!" "Make a bee-line for our new books!"

Start with a large, egg shaped styrofoam ball painted yellow. Paint black strips around the back end, which is the smaller more pointed end. Black electrical tape will work also if you don't want to paint the stripes.

Use a very small styrofoam ball cut in half. Glue these halves on for eyes and paint them black. Use a black pipe cleaner for each antenna.

Take three black pipe cleaners and cut each in half. Fold each piece to make a leg. Insert three on each side of the bumblebee body.

Use white wire or white pipe cleaners glued to wax paper to make the four wings. After they are completely dry, twist two of

Wax Paper

the wing pieces together. Insert one of the wing sections into each side of the bee.

Hang your little bee from the ceiling with fishing line to buzz around your paper flowers.

Pots of flowers

So, were the previous ideas just too time consuming or too much work? Well, create some pots of flowers with personality. Use some clay pots with floral stryofoam inside covered up with Spanish moss. For each flower you will need a thin dowel rod painted green for the stem. Tape on a flower face with petals, a couple of leaves and a paper book. These will fit in just about anywhere.

Is It Spring Yet?

This can be done as a display by itself or added to the garden theme. Frogs are fun and popular with children. Combine them with some kites to fly around the room. Make a pattern out of newspaper. Trace your pattern onto green posterboard and cut it out. Use a black marker to draw in the details of your frog. Fold the legs in the three places shown in the drawing so that the legs will swing as the frog is flying around on the kite. The frogs will be hanging around your room bringing a smile to everyone who comes in.

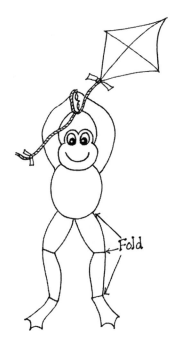

Fold

Or, how about a jumping frog holding a book with the phrase: "A day without reading makes me jumpy!"

Hoppy Spring!

The Farm

Kids for years have loved the song "Old Macdonald Had a Farm." Use this idea to decorate the whole library by featuring all aspects of the farm and some of the animals found there.

The barn is the focal point of the farm. Use some large, red poster paper to create the building. Make it to fit the bulletin board or even better, make it to fit an entire wall.

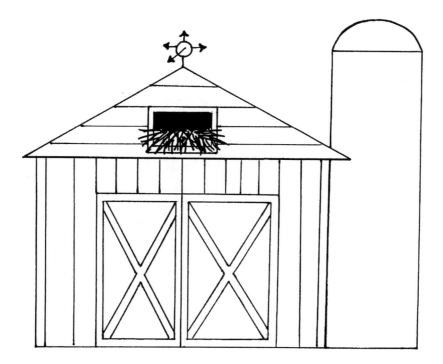

Basically the building is just a large rectangle with a triangle for the roof section. Create a loft window by gluing on a small black rectangle. Use rafia or some yellow construction paper cut in small strips or straw that hangs out of the loft window.

Use a black marker to draw in the door area. Cut some thin strips of white paper. Glue them on criss-crossed in the door area and add some on each end of the building and the loft window as trim. Use black paper to create some simple type of weathervane for the top of the barn. Depending on how much you want to do, consider adding a fence, maybe a rain barrel, or a wagon wheel.

Use some gray construction paper to make the silo. It is just a long, thin rectangle with a semi-circle for the top. Add some details with a black marker.

Turn a table into a wagon display of books. Cut four wheels, each the size of a sheet of posterboard. Since brown is not a common color for posterboard, go with black. Cut these with spokes to look like old wooden wagon wheels.

If you have access to some bales of straw, use them on the table top as a display space. (Cover the table top with plastic before you add the straw. This will aid in clean up later.) Pile up the bales of straw to create some height to the display. Place books about farms, farm animals, fiction stories about farms, and even books like *Hank the Cowdog* or *Click, Clack, Moo: Cows That Type*, around the table at varying heights.

If you don't have access to bales of straw, use boxes piled up. Cover them with a plastic tablecloth or an old quilt and add the books. Add a long paper banner with a message like "A Harvest of Great Titles."

Now, the barn is just a building. It's the animals that will give your display some life. Add lots of cows, chickens, pigs, sheep, and ducks.

And on this farm, Old Macdonald had some cows. Make a big cow head in black and white paper to go with some appropriate words.

Make some smaller 3-D cows out of posterboard or construction paper that can be set among the books in a display. Draw the pattern on to a folded piece of posterboard with the top of the cow along the fold. Cut out the cow while the paper is still folded.

Use markers to draw in all the details and to make your cow a Holstein. All cows are not black and white but these are pretty funny for displays. You decide on the color.

Consider putting a cute cow with these words: "Have you seen the moo-oovie? Read the book!"

And on this farm, Old Macdonald had some chickens. Use chickens to help you promote some "eggs-cellent" chapter books. To accompany a farm theme, consider a display of chapter books of varying difficulty levels and subject matter. This bulletin board could be just what you need.

Use a bright blue background with black or dark blue lettering. The chickens should be white or brown with touches of red and yellow. Don't worry about making realistic chickens. Rather funny looking chickens will be very appealing to your students. Add some egg shapes with the names of some chapter books written on them. Be sure to include the call numbers.

And on this farm, Old Macdonald had some pigs. Pigs make us laugh. Let your pigs "ham it up" and bring some fun to your farm display. The pigs can hold their own as the center of a bulletin board or position them among books in a display.

Make some large pigs cut out of cardboard. Paint them pink and trim up the details in black. Just use an opaque projector to enlarge one of the pig patterns included. These can be taped to a bookend to be able to stand freely on the top of a bookshelf.

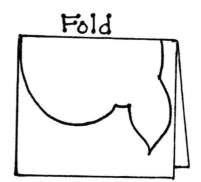

Another option would be to just make the head and two front feet of the pig. Fold a sheet of 12" × 18" pink construction paper in half the short way. Draw half of the head on the fold. Cut this out while the paper is still folded.

Open this up to reveal the pig's head. Use a black marker to add the eyes, snout, and mouth. If you would prefer, the eyes and mouth could be

cut from construction paper and glued on.

Fold a 9" × 12" piece of paper in half. Draw on a foot. Cut the feet out while the paper is still folded so that you will have two feet exactly the same. You will, of course, have to flip one over to have a right and left.

Make some construction paper books or use real book jackets or magazines on the bulletin board. Position the head and hands to make it look like the pig is reading. Add an appropriate phrase.

Some standing pigs would look great tucked in places around the room. Use a piece of 12" × 18" construction paper folded in half the short way to create a 9" × 12" side to work with. Draw on the pig pattern and cut out the pig while the paper is still folded.

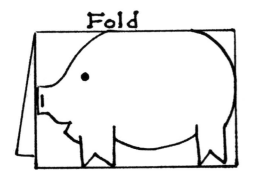

Add two ears. Cut the paper as in the illustration. Fold a pleat in the bottom of the ear and staple the ear to the pig. Cut a thin 6" strip of pink paper and then roll it around a pencil. Glue it on for the tail. Use a black marker for any additional details.

And on the farm Old Macdonald had some sheep. Sheep are pretty easy to make. The sheep's body is very much like a fluffy cloud. Use white paper or posterboard and you might consider adding polyester fiberfill for some fluff.

Use black construction paper for the face, one ear, and four legs. The face is an oval. The ear can be cut from the scraps of the oval. Fold the ear down the middle to make it stick out some when it is glued down. For the legs, fold

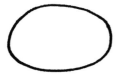

a large sheet of black paper into fourths and draw your pattern on the top section. Cut all four legs at the same time.

Add a phrase like: "Ewe should be reading!"

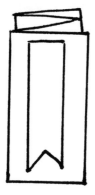

These would be great to use with some books like *Bad Boys* or *Betsy Who Cried Wolf.*

Add a rocking chair to the library if possible. Imagine sitting on the porch of the old farm house rocking and reading.

If possible, add some quilts or quilt designs in the room. Consider making a nine patch quilt with the blocks made of construction paper. Write in the titles of farm related books in the squares. Randomly add a small picture of a pig, cow, chicken, etc. The finished paper quilt could be hung on the wall. Go ahead and give it a blue ribbon from the county fair.

And on this farm Old Macdonald had some ducks.

Feature some cartoon-like ducks reading in various poses. Make the duck bodies from white paper using a black marker to add the details. Use yellow or orange paper for the beak and feet outlining the parts in black marker.

3-D ducks sitting and reading can be made from brown grocery bags.

Stuff the bag with newspaper and close it tightly with a rubber band. Fluff up the end to create a tail feather area. Paint the bag white.

Use heavy posterboard to create the neck and head of the duck. If the head is too floppy, glue a strip of heavy cardboard painted white along the

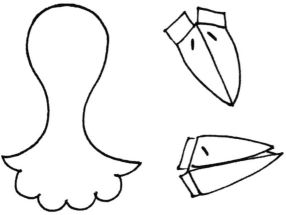

neck extending up to the head.

Use orange or bright yellow posterboard or construction paper for the beak. The beak is made up of two pieces with each piece folded down the middle to

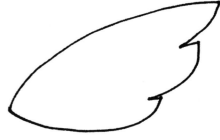

make it stand out and give the 3-D look. Glue these on to the head.

Make two wings that can be positioned around a book.

"Leaf" It to the Library

Lots of red, yellow, orange, and brown in a display means it must be autumn. The fall is such a beautiful time of the year and the time to feature leaves and great books.

Use a variety of leaf shapes. Try one of the patterns included or use some real leaves as your patterns. Also, use a variety of media. Construction paper is probably your first choice, but consider some colored cellophane or tissue paper.

Cut a variety of leaves in red, orange, yellow, and brown and staple them together to create a leaf chain. Drape this new garland around your door. Tie

up the corners with a bow made from burlap strips or some coarse ribbon in a fall color. Add some Indian corn to the ribbon bows if possible.

Make some leaf silhouettes using black construction paper. Holding two pieces of paper, cut out two leaves exactly the same. On one sheet cut out shapes within the leaf. Lay this down on the other leaf and using a pencil, trace these new shapes. Cut them out of the second sheet. Slide a piece of colored cellophane between the two black leaves. Carefully glue them together. Hang these at varying lengths with fishing line. Hang them close to windows if possible for the extra light to maximize their potential beauty.

Make some large construction paper leaves of various colors to slide in the top of books you are featuring. Just cut a long slit up the middle so that you can position it in the book. Laminate them if possible. Add a message such as: "This book is so scary!!!"

This book is so scary!!

109

Put a simple banner on the wall with a message like: "Leaf" through one of our new books."

Scarecrows are traditional fall icons. Create one of your own using some old clothes, a brown paper bag, some newspaper, and a lawn chair. If you don't have room for a seated scarecrow, make one that can lounge and read out of the way on the top of a bookcase.

You will need a yardstick for the spine and a ruler for the collarbone. Tape them or tie them together. Draw a face on the brown bag with markers and then stuff the bag half full with newspapers.

Slide the bag over the top of the yardstick and tie the bag closed. Position a shirt on the ruler and button up the front. Stuff this and the sleeves with newspaper. Stuff a pair of gloves with newspaper for the hands and slide them in the bottom of the shirt cuffs and pin them in place. Use an old pair of jeans stuffed with newspaper and stuff the legs into the top of a pair of old boots or high-topped tennis shoes. Put the shirt into the pants and position the body into the lawn chair. You may have to tie the scarecrow to the chair to keep it sitting correctly.

Add some straw or a wig for hair and a floppy old hat. A bandana around the neck would cover the bottom of the bag. Position the gloves to hold a book and place some other books around the chair.

A Reading Tree

Create a wonderful reading spot in your library with a floor-to-ceiling tree. Begin with a carpet tube that is approximately six feet tall. Position the tube on a base as described earlier in this book and screw it in place. This will serve as the armature for the tree.

Use the long strips of brown mailing paper that come as packing material these days. If you don't have access to some of this, use the brown mailing paper that comes on a roll. This will be the bark of the tree and will form the limbs. Staple one end of the paper strip to the bottom of the carpet tube. Crumple and twist the paper and loosely wrap the strip around the tube. Secure the end and begin again by overlapping a new piece. Continue this process until the trunk is all covered. Add more paper to make the trunk fatter.

Twisted brown paper strips form the branches. Use fishing line hanging down from the ceiling to support these branches. Add leaves and even some apples for extra color. Use green fabric around the base to cover the boards and act as the grass. Position a lawn chair in front of the tree as your place to sit when you read to the children.

If you don't want to go to all this work, just hang a tree limb from the ceiling. Consider adding a string of lights to make the display more dramatic. As the seasons change, vary the foliage. In the winter, hang some snowflakes.

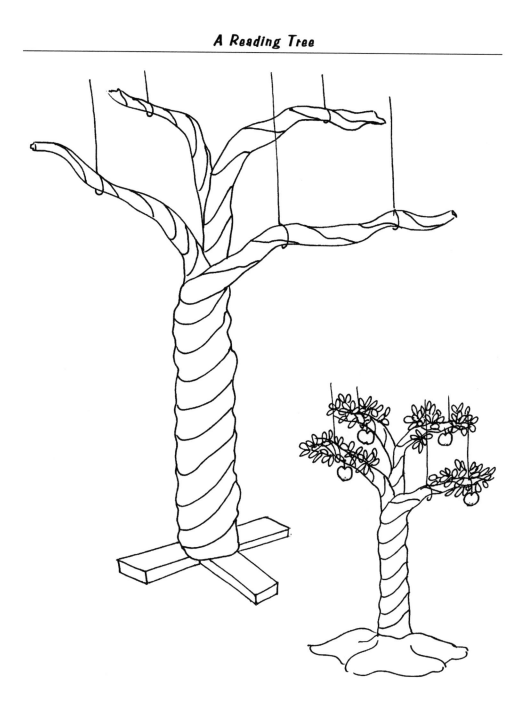

Let's Go Camping

The idea of camping out and the freedom of the great outdoors is very appealing. Use this theme to showcase some of your books on nature, animals native to your area, outdoor safety, and survival skills.

If you have a small pup tent, set it up in an out-of-the-way spot to create a fun "reading room." If not, create a little homemade tent with a blanket and a rope. Use other camping items around the room, such as a sleeping bag or two, and even a lantern. Use a pair of boots as bookends or a pencil holder. If you have access to stuffed animals that would fit this theme, position them with books around the room.

A campfire is always a must. This would be terrific for the children to sit around for storytime. Use short pieces of carpet tube for the logs. Cover the whole tube, including the ends, with brown paper. Use a brown or black marker to draw in some lines to simulate wood grain. Use colored cellophane or red and orange construction paper to create the flames. If you have access to some large rocks, circle the campfire with them. To finish off the look, include a camp stool for you to sit on when you read to the children.

Little white lights hung across the ceiling can be the stars one would see in the wide open spaces. Also feature a length of lights as a border for a bulletin board featuring owls.

Make three sizes of reading owls from construction paper. Position them in a row on the tree limb. Keep them simple and just use markers to draw in the details. Start with a 9" × 12" piece of construction paper. Add an orange diamond shaped beak, two eyes, and some orange claw feet. Just make a small, medium, and large version of the same owl.

Some 3-D owls would look awesome sitting in different area of the library. They might be reading or holding signs. These can be made by taking a 12" × 18"

sheet of brown or gray paper. Draw on the pattern. Use a crayon or marker to draw some feathers on the bottom half of the shape. Cut out the shape and staple it into a circle.

To make the beak, use a square of yellow paper. Fold the top and bottom to the center, leaving a small strip in the middle. This area is what will be glued onto the owl. The beak will stick out from the background. Glue on two black circles for eyes.

Cut two wings at the same time. Glue these on and position them to hold a book or a sign. Add a pair of orange claw feet.

Create an easy bulletin board by using a large sheet of blue paper for the background. Use book covers or create books out of construction paper. Add trunks so that you now have trees. Add a stripe of green paper along the bottom and place the newly designed trees in any order or placement that you would like.

For a border, make a silhouette of a bear. Position these bears as though they are following each other across the board.

Add a phrase such as: "Big Skies...Big Reading."

A moose head hanging on the wall would add another touch of the great outdoors. Create a humorous version

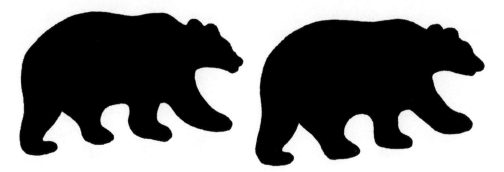

using a brown paper bag stuffed with newspaper. Close up the bag by twisting the top and fastening it with a rubber band. Add some eyes and nostrils. Use brown paper to make the ears and the antlers. Glue all this on a piece of cardboard to hang on the wall.

Check your reference books for animal tracks. Make some from construction paper and have them lead the way around the room. Ask the children to identify the tracks.

Contact your local conservation office and schedule a visit from one of the animal experts. Many times they will bring an animal display, do bird calls, or just share their love for the outdoors.

Gone Readin'

If you can't go fishing, create a humorous fishing scene in your library. Bring in an empty tacklebox, some fishing poles, and a dip net to add to the fishing mood.

Diary of a Worm

Get hooked on reading.

Blue paper works well for the background. Use some brown chalk or a brown crayon to color in some dirt in the bottom. This doesn't need to be solid area of color but just the hint of dirt. Add some green grass.

Or, for a different look, you might consider using a piece of blue plastic. Open up a blue plastic trash bag or even use a blue plastic tarp for the background. The great thing about the blue plastic is that it has a nice shine and the plastic will move slightly with breezes and this will give the display more life.

The number of fish is up to you. Keep the fish relatively simple. Light brown or light green would be good fish colors. If you use yellow or orange, your fish might look like goldfish. The fish body is really just a football shape. Add some construction paper or tissue paper fins and use a marker to finish up the other details such as the eye and mouth.

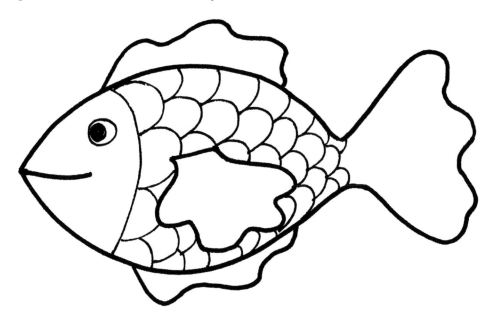

Position a piece of bamboo or a cane fishing pole with some fishing line tied to it to dangle your construction paper worm in front of the bulletin board. Be sure to make a book for that worm. *Diary of a Worm* would be a great choice for worm reading material and it is a popular book with children.

Open up the tacklebox and place a book or two on it and in it. Put a book in the dip net and set it in the midst of some books. Add a sign on the wall or hang a sign from another fishing pole.

A whole underwater theme can be done by expanding to saltwater wildlife, shells, crabs, seahorses, etc. A possible phrase might be: "Let's dive into a good book ... 'shell' we?

Thirsty for a Good Book?

Go with a whole "thirsty" theme. Only reading will be able to quench this thirst. For this bulletin board idea, use blue paper for the background with a giant sun complete with yellow and orange rays.

For the glass, use a piece of lamination film that has been laminated. This will provide for a clear glass so that the sun will show through, along with construction paper book ice cubes and a straw. Use a black permanent marker to outline the glass and each item in it.

Position the glass on a construction paper book. Add some letters in a bold contrasting color.

Check the teacher's lounge for some empty soda cans. Use your computer to print up some new labels for these washed out cans. You can create a refreshing can of Fiction, Mystery, etc. Set these among a display of books.

Or, consider setting up a desert-like area complete with a big cactus. Use a piece of a carpet tube for the trunk of the cactus and duct tape it to a piece of board or heavy cardboard for the base. Drop a rock or two in the tube to make it bottom heavy. A base can even be made similar to the one suggested for the palm tree in an earlier chapter. (If you have extra money to spend, PVC pipe can be used for the armature.)

Cut small sections of carpet tube for the arms of the cactus. Duct tape these on with newspaper stuffed in for the elbow bend to tie them together. When the armature is complete, cover the whole thing with papier-mâché. Strips of newspaper dipped in wallpaper paste work well.

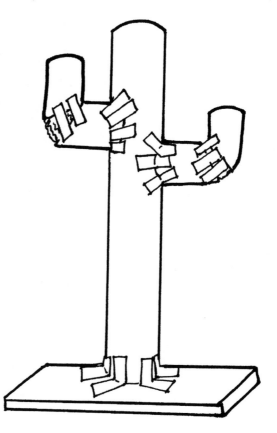

After it dries, use a nail to punch in some small holes evenly all over the cactus. Paint the cactus green and when it is dry, insert ½ of a toothpick in each hole. Dip the toothpick in glue as you insert it to keep it in place.

To accompany your cactus in a display, use some tan fabric for your sand and include a cow skull, if available, or a rubber snake. Hang a large piece of posterboard behind the cactus with some refreshing words.

Take a Walk on the Wild Side

In the 500s, the Science section, decorate around the bookshelves that hold books about the rain forest, snakes, lizards, monkeys, spiders, etc. Your patrons will be surprised to find a display in an out-of-the-way place. Cover the background wall with black paper or hang some from the ceiling to create a partition if the bookshelf is not against the wall. Use white or yellow paper for the letters. Cut out some eyes from yellow or green and glue them on to this dark background as though the eyes of some animals are peering out through the darkness.

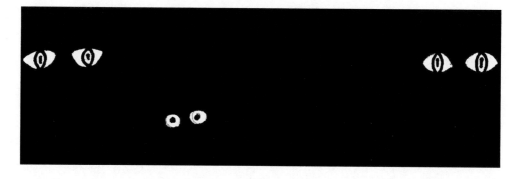

Create some vines from green ribbon with tissue paper leaves. Thin green ribbon is very inexpensive and comes on a roll that is about ten yards long. Cut the leaves while the paper is folded so that you can cut many at a time.

Fold the bottom edges as in the illustration and staple the leaf to the ribbon. This fold will make the leaf stand out and be stronger.

Hang the vine from the ceiling and along the top of the bookshelves. Add some wildlife. Whatever you feel comfortable making will be great.

A spider made from a sweet gum ball seed pod will be very attention getting. Glue a small black pompon on to the gumball for the spider's head. Add a pair of small roll-around eyes.

Use four black fuzzy pipecleaners cut in half and bent to form the legs.

Glue the legs by putting glue in the holes of the seed pod and inserting the leg into the hole. Glue a piece of elastic thread to the top of the seed pod. Let this all dry thoroughly.

Dangle the spider from the vine so that it is out of the traffic flow and high enough to not be bumped, but very visible. Use a white pencil, white crayon, or white chalk to add a web to the black background paper.

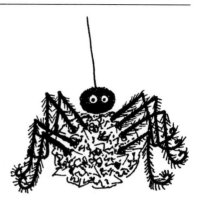

A snake can be made from a piece of plastic hose with a styrofoam ball duct taped on the end of the hose for the head. Paint the snake in a cool design. If the hose is flexible enough, coil and bend the snake as you position it among the vines.

A great monkey can be made from cardboard and hung on the vines or the edge of the bookshelf. Enlarge the pattern included and draw it on some heavy cardboard. Cut out the monkey and paint it a warm brown color. Use a black permanent marker to add the details.

Pirates

For this bulletin board, use some brown mailing paper for the background. Crumple it up and tear along the edges so that it will look as though it is very old.

Keep your pirate very simple. Humorous and cartoon-like is great. Who needs scary anyway? All you really need is a head and two hands. Copy the

pirate head pattern onto a sheet of 9" × 12" construction paper. On the same color construction paper, trace around your hands for the pirate's hands. These will be attached to the telescope. The viewer's eye can connect the hands to the pirate in his mind.

Use construction paper to create your telescope. The telescope can be flat or 3-D. Roll the paper into tubes and just create three sizes. Tape the smaller one into the next larger and so forth. Hold the scope up to your eye to see exactly where to glue the paper hands on. Position them just as you are holding the telescope. Add a circle of paper in the end of the scope with the word "READ" written on it.

On your background, add the words you choose and be sure to include a big "X" with the words "The Library" written next to it. Add some dotted lines to show the route to the treasure.

If you decide to add a pirate flag to your display, add a book for your Jolly Roger to be reading. A parrot stuffed animal would top everything off!

To make a 3-D treasure chest, start with a box that has a lid. A box that copy machine paper comes in would work well if you have a space big enough for that. Cover the box with brown paper. Use a black or brown marker to draw in the lines to simulate wood. Add a strip of black construction paper on each corner. This will contrast nicely with the brown paper and make the box look much more finished.

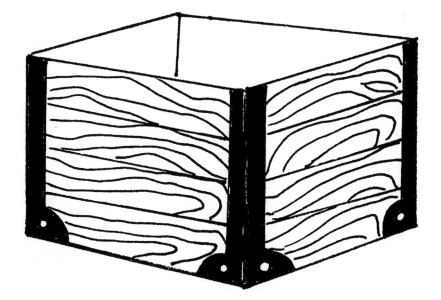

For the lid, cover it in brown paper following the same directions. If you want your chest to be closed, put the lid on the box like normal. Add two black construction paper strips to simulate the hinges. Add a lock area made from black construction paper. Glue on some "jewels" or shapes cut from foil paper.

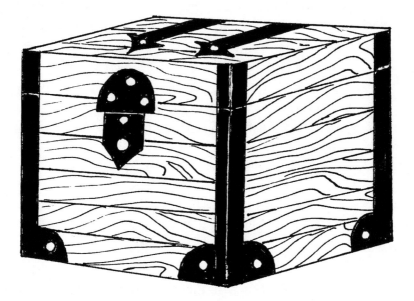

If your trunk is open, position the lid how you would like it to be. Tape it in place on the inside and use black construction paper for your hinges. If these don't hold, use some cardboard strips covered in black paper. If all else fails, stand a piece of cardboard inconspicuously inside to hold the lid open.

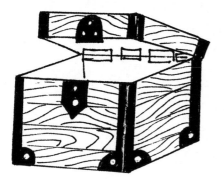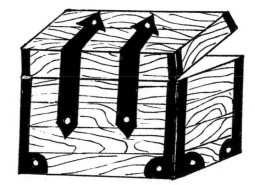

Fill the box with gold or silver foil paper, fake gold coins, and strings of old beads. Include a book or two since that is the real treasure. Add an accompanying sign on what looks like a treasure map: "Opening a book is like opening a treasure chest!"

Pencils

Students use pencils every day and they would enjoy seeing some super-sized pencils hanging in the library. These can be personalized to fit your school. They are definitely attention-getters and are great to use to point the way to the pencil sharpener or to specific areas of the library, such as the biographies, fiction, and other areas.

You will need a carpet tube. Cut the tube with a saw to the desired length. To make the eraser ends, first cover the end of the tube with clear tape to close it off. Pull a sheet of 9" × 12" pink construction paper over the end of the tube. Carefully fold down the paper and tape it in place.

Wrap a sheet of pink paper around the tube so that the pleats and tape are covered and the straight edge of the paper forms the edge of the eraser. Staple or glue this in place.

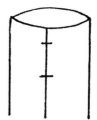

The point end of the pencil is the trickiest part. Roll a 12" × 18" sheet of pink construction paper into a cone that fits the end of the tube and staple it together. Use a black marker to color in the lead for your pencil. Cover this black area with clear tape to create a shine that a real sharpened pencil point has.

Fill the cone tightly with small wads of newspaper. This will help the cone to keep its shape and to protect it from being squished if bumped. Slide the cone on to the tube. Smooth the edges down and tape it to the tube.

Choose any color of paper for the middle section. You might use the school colors or try some wild wrapping paper design. Be sure to measure correctly because this will be a large piece of paper. You won't want to have to patch it. Wrap the paper around the tube, creating a straight edge along the pink on the point end. Don't worry about the eraser end being perfect. Use silver paper or aluminum foil trimmed with a black marker for the ferrule of the pencil. Glue this on around the pencil and it will give the eraser end that finished look and a cool shine.

Complete the process by adding some words. Cut the letters from construction paper and glue them on. You might think that it would be faster to just write the word on in marker. But. ...what if you make a mistake or your writing is sloppy? After all the work you've done to make the pencil, finish it up well with nice letters.

Use some heavy strength fishing line to hang your pencil. Just use two pieces of string to create a sling and slide the pencil in.

Pencils can also be put across the top of a bookshelf or you can lean them in a corner with the point end up. Consider hanging one in the hall to point the way to the library. Make the pencils of your display different lengths for some variety. Be creative and enjoy your handiwork!

Library Building Blocks

Create ten blocks—one for each area of the Dewey Decimal System. On one side of the block put the number, on one side the name of the area, and write in subject headings for that particular Dewey area on the remaining spaces. Add pictures of the different subjects to make the blocks more colorful and interesting.

Stack these up in a creative display. This could become the library pyramid. The Dewey system is the building block of library organization. Additional boxes could be made to spell out the word "Library."

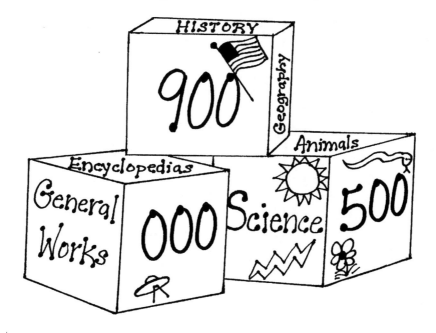

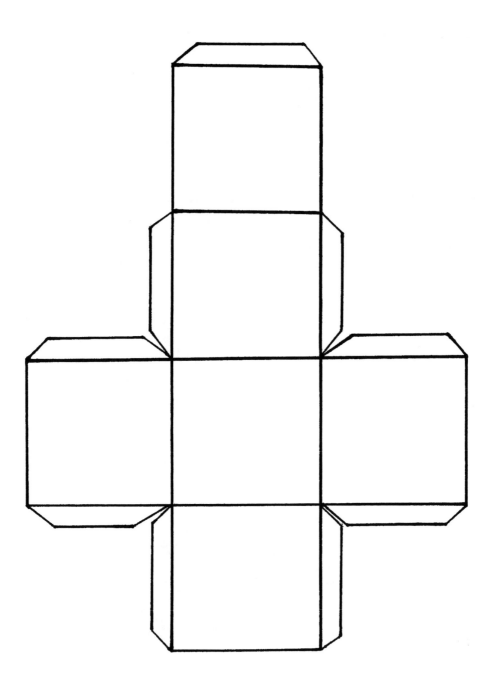

Exercise

The talk these days is about the need for us to exercise more. Our brains also need to exercise and one great way is by reading more.

Create a version of your school mascot sitting in a big chair enjoying a good book. This would be a terrific attention-getting display when paired with the phrase "Exercise your brain ... READ!"

Make some construction paper books complete with arms and legs. These should look very cartoon-like. Position them doing all types of exercising from weightlifting to skateboarding. Just have fun with them. Place them in out of the way spots throughout the library and with some books on nutrition and all types of sports.

Don't "weight"—read today!   Race to read!

Jump into an adventure book!

Push yourself to read more books.

Run to the library.

Get pumped for reading.

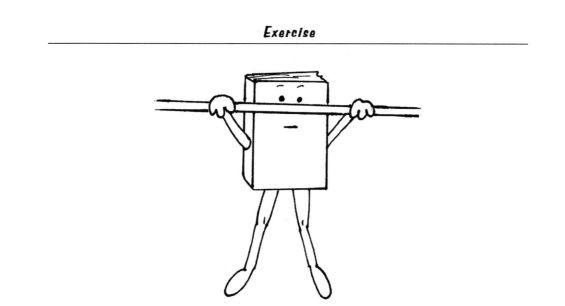

Hang on ... the new books are here!

Jump Right into a Good Book!

Do you need a small display to fill an odd space? Borrow a couple of jump ropes from your coach. Stretch one out in your display space and use others to wrap around some books. Add letters to finish up this easy to make display. This would be great for books on fitness and exercise.

Get in Step ... Read!

If you need a bulletin board that is quick to make and is oh, so easy, try this. Choose a bright color for the long rectangular background and a bold color for the letters. Use the phrase suggested or try one such as: "Lead the way to the new books" or "Follow the leader to the new books."

Use real shoes, such as flip flops, along the bottom of the bulletin board as though they were walking along. You need to use shoes that have soles that a pin can go through to attach the shoe to the bulletin board.

If you are not using a bulletin board and there is no way to physically

attach a real shoe, just create some construction paper flip flops. Either trace around a real flip flop or use the pattern provided. Photocopy the pattern onto some color of construction paper.

For the straps, use a 9" × 12" piece of construction paper. Fold the paper in half. Trace around the strap pattern which is included with the shoe pattern. Cut it out while the paper is still folded.

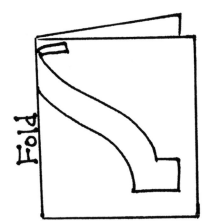

Cut a 2" piece of a colored plastic straw. Fit this piece into the X on the shoe pattern. Tape it in on the back side. Slide the strap piece with the center point into the piece of straw. Glue it in place.

Slip the ends of the strap into the slits on the sides of the sandal. Tape them from the back. Decorate the straps by coloring them, adding stripes, or by just gluing on "jewels" or other ornamentation.

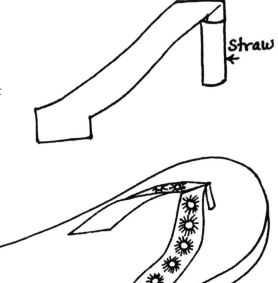

142

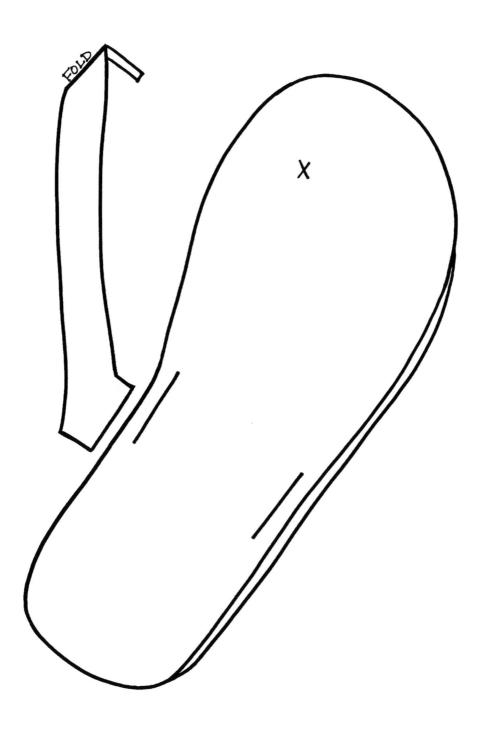

To carry the shoe theme a little further, use shoes to hold pencils, as paper weights, or even use a rubber-soled shoe as a planter. Fill some old hightop shoes with rocks to serve as bookends.

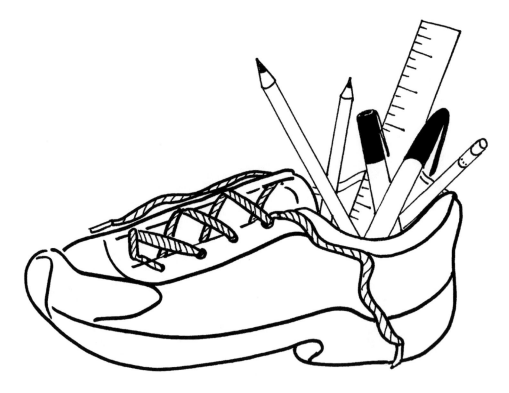

Money

Create a large, pink piggybank that is enjoying a good book. Pull out all those books in the economics section that no one ever looks at. Dust them off! Print up some signs that ask questions like "How much do you know about money?" "Where does our money come from?" "How is our money made?" "Why does our money look like it does?"

Reading... it just makes cents ¢

¢

Knowledge is like money in the bank!

To add a little pizzazz to the display and to make it more three dimensional, make some large coins from posterboard. Use the patterns included and an opaque projector to create your own giant coins. Hang these at varying lengths with fishing line. Include some dollar and cent signs.

Good Book Cafe

Turn your bulletin board into a cafe window. Create an awning from poster paper or even a plastic tablecloth. Plain or striped will work just fine. Attach the top edge of the paper to the wall close to the ceiling. Fold the front edge toward the top to form a casing. Tape it in place.

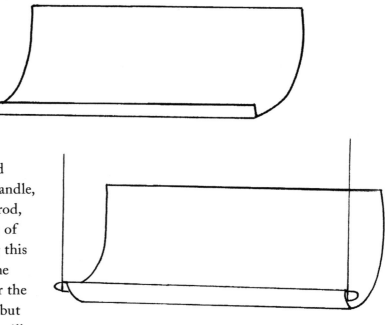

Slide in a dowel rod, yard stick, broom handle, round curtain rod, or even a piece of bamboo. Hang this with fishing line positioned over the bulletin board but so that no one will run into it.

Cover the background of the bulletin board with black paper using white or yellow for the lettering. Create a list of some of your new books with the title, author, and call number. Print this on your computer but do make the type large enough to be read easily.

If you have the time and the red paper, you can add brickwork around your new window. Cut pieces of red paper in 3" × 6" pieces and put them on the wall as though you were really laying bricks. You will, of course, have to cut some of them in half to keep the pattern going, but it will look great and make the window bulletin board look a little more like a window.

Position a table and two chairs near the awning as though you are ready for actual diners. Cover the table with a tablecloth, and why not add a candle or some flowers? Set some books on the table to entice your readers. You have just created a lovely outdoor cafe. Bon appetite!

Recipe for a Great Book Report

For a great tabletop display, use a real mixing bowl with a spoon, some measuring cups, and any other equipment you want to add. To add a little humor, cover an empty oatmeal box or cereal box with some colorful paper. On your computer, print a label for "Fiction" plus some promises such as "Guaranteed to give you hours of enjoyment." Glue the label on the box. The same could be done for nonfiction and other areas. Set these on a checkered tablecloth.

Choose some books for the display and put one inside the bowl. Create a chef's hat to sit on top of another book.

A chef's hat is easy to make. Cut a long strip of white posterboard and fold it in half lengthwise. Make the fold very sharp. This will become the band of the hat. Form the unfolded band into a circle and staple once along the top section where the ends overlap. Leave the bottom half open to make it easier to fold it up later.

Cut a very large circle of white tissue paper. This will become the top of the hat and will be pleated and attached to the band with tape.

Carefully pleat the large tissue paper circle around the unfolded band. Tape the tissue paper down securely but be sure the tape does not extend higher than the top of the band.

Fold the band up to cover the tape. Staple the band together to close it up. Fluff the top of the hat and it is ready for use.

Use a piece of white posterboard with the corners rounded to create a recipe card. Hang the card with fishing line behind the display or stick it to the wall if possible.

T-Shirts with Library Style

T-shirts are a major part of any child's wardrobe. Create some library T-shirts to advertise some new books or books on a particular subject.

Begin with sheets of posterboard in different colors. You will need one piece for each book you want to feature. Create a pattern on a sheet of newspaper so that all your shirts will be the same size.

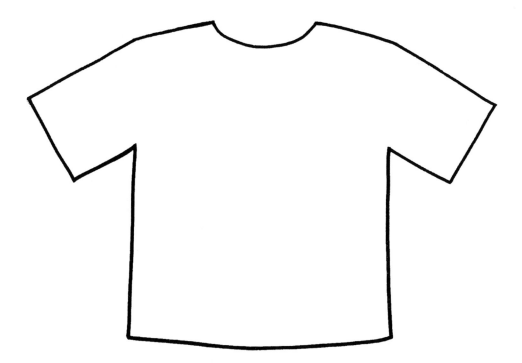

Trace around your pattern and cut out the shirt. Take a digital photo of a book, print off the picture, and glue it some place on the shirt. Use a black marker to write in a short book review plus the title, author, and call number. This is a wonderful way to have your students do a book review and create their own special "library" T-shirt.

Hang these T-shirts on a pretend clothesline with clothespins. The unused display area across a set of windows would be a great place for this clothesline. Stretch a lightweight rope across the area and secure both ends. If a clothesline won't work for you, tape the shirt to a hanger. Hang up the "laundry" around the room and create an awesome display.

Add to this idea by using laundry baskets to hold some of the new books or other items around the room. Team these up with an ironing board for an additional unique book display space.

Socks

Use real socks of varying colors along with a display of new books or books on a specific subject. (This is a good opportunity to do something with those mismatched socks in your laundry.) Use tissue paper to stuff the socks to give them some shape.

This will work well as a bulletin board or as just a display on the top of a bookshelf. Hang some socks and let the books wear some.

Our new books will knock your socks off!

Welcome Back

Start the year with a display of a big yellow school bus complete with photos of your faculty members reading some of your new books.

Begin with a large sheet of yellow poster paper. Think really big! Cut out a bus shape and add two black construction paper tires. Glue on some large blue squares for the window areas. Take digital photos of your faculty members reading books and print them. Glue these photos on the blue squares to look like these teachers are on the bus reading. Be sure to pose them so they will face the front of your bus. Use a photo of the librarian or the school mascot to pose as the driver.

Need a Hand?

Start with a black or dark color background. Use a white pencil to write in familiar library "stuff." Trace around your hand. Use an opaque projector to enlarge your hand drawing to a size that fills up the center of your

Encyclopedias, Atlases, Science, Language, Art, Geography, Travel, Dinosaurs, Internet, Mathematics Chemistry Military, Health Biographies, Poetry, Fairy Tales, Mystery Adventure, Newspapers, DVDs Fantasy, Fiction, Nonfiction, History Videos, Cookbooks, Holidays Dictionaries.

Need a hand? Just ask for help.

display space. Cut out the hand shape and position it in place. Use a bright color for the letters to call attention to your message.

The hand idea can be expanded to create a wreath for the door. Use lots of colors of construction paper and don't limit yourself to just normal skin colors. Go wild!

Arrange the hand shapes in a circle and tape them to the door. Add black construction paper letters to spell out the word "Welcome." Finish up by adding a big ribbon or paper bow.

Use work gloves, dress gloves, and even mittens filled with tissue paper to point out things in your library or to point the way to your book display. Give yourself a hand for putting together a great display!

Cowboys

What do you think of the old song that says, "Mamas, don't let your babies grow up to be cowboys"? People are fascinated by the Old West and the lore of the cowboy. Build on this theme by featuring cowboy hats, boots, horseshoes, a lasso, and even a saddle if you have one.

Set up a display of books on cowboys in fact and fiction. Use a rope and lasso one while wrapping the remainder of the rope around several others. Add some appropriate words to the wall area behind the books. Pose a cowboy hat sitting on the top of a book or tie on a bandana.

Horseshoes are symbolic of good luck. Make some giant cardboard ones to hang around. Add a sign such as: "No luck needed here in finding a good book. All our books are winners!"

Do some research on authentic brands. Use some of these around the room. Add these to a sign that says something like: "Need a good book? We have all brands here."

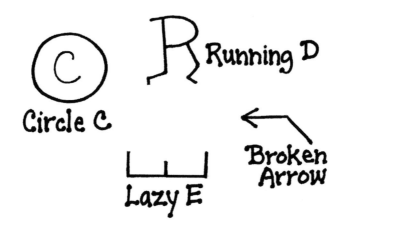

Make some wanted posters of some of your students' favorite authors. Try to keep the look rather old, rather antique, and just plain humorous. These could be printed on the computer and used for a bulletin board or to just decorate a wall area. Include a sign with an appropriate message such as: "Wanted ... good readers for our great books!"

Use an old pair of boots to serve as a planter. An old boot can also be used to hold pencils, etc. Stuff paper in the shoe to fill up space so that the pencils don't fall down inside too far.

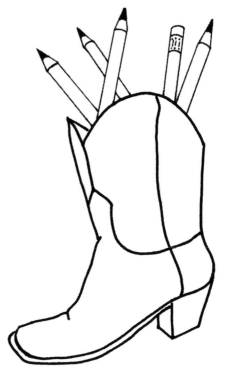

Make Time to Read a Good Book

Create a giant watch from poster paper. Use the Dewey Decimal areas for the watch numbers. Laminate the watch face to act as the watch crystal and to add that special shine.

Use bright, contrasting colors to give this display a fun feeling. Consider bright yellow for the background with a red watchband and black lettering.

Use this display as a learning tool by asking your students what time it is and what they might find in that Dewey area. If it is 1:33, they just might find a ghost book or 8:11 could be a great poetry book.

Make time to read a good book today!

Fiction 000   100
92   200
900   300
800   400
700 600 500

Standard Dewey Time.

Just watch what will happen!

We've Gone Batty for Books

For this display with a 3-D element, begin with a black or dark blue background with a large yellow or orange moon. This needs to be a significantly large circle to provide the needed color for the display. Use white letters, which will really pop on the dark background. Trim the edges nicely so that no border will be needed.

Display any type of books with this idea. The first thought would be that this is just a Halloween display, but it would serve well for a display of books about nocturnal animals or really anything.

The bats are very easy to make. Although they may be made any size, the average bat works well made from a 9" × 12" piece of black construction paper.

Fold the piece of paper in half. Draw a pencil line about an inch from the fold. This will be the body area of the bat.

Use a pencil to draw in half of the bat on the fold. Cut out the bat while the paper is still folded.

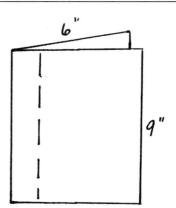

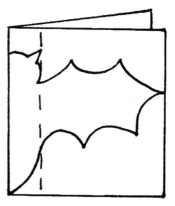

Glue the body section together and fold down the wings. Hang the bats with fishing line.

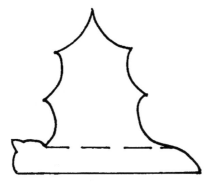

As they move when the breeze hits them, your display will come to life.

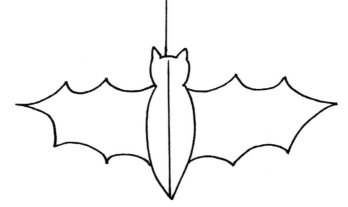

Read a Good
BOO-OOK Today

Use black or dark blue paper for the background. Cut a large yellow circle for the moon.

Use waxed paper for your ghosts. The neat thing about these ghosts is that they are fairly transparent but still quite sturdy. Use a black marker to draw on the eyes and mouth or glue on black construction paper features. Make the ghosts different sizes and overlap them so it appears they are sharing the same book.

Use a real book or make up one of your own from construction paper. Another good phrase for this display would be: "Share a good BOO-OOK with a friend."

Accessorize!

Accessorize! That's the fashionable thing to do. Well, accessorize with a good book. It will go with any outfit on any day.

A good book....
the perfect
accessory!

To make this display, use real fashion items. If you don't want to use your own hat, purse, shoes, belt, etc., pick up some wild choices at a thrift store or garage sale. Nothing needs to match and it certainly doesn't need to be new. Choose a feminine color background such as purple or hot pink to set off this conglomeration of items.

Choose a variety of books to showcase. Spread some of your accessories around these books like a belt or tying a scarf around a book. Keep the whole display light and fun. Feathered boas are certainly welcome!

Catch the Vision

Create some giant glasses and sunglasses. Make these from posterboard if you want to hang them. If you just plan to place them on the wall, poster paper will work just fine.

Use the pattern provided and enlarge it with an opaque projector. Cut out the pieces and assemble them with staples and glue. For the clear lens, use lamination film that has gone through the laminator or clear cellophane. Use colored cellophane for sunglasses lenses. Adding letters to the lens to spell "READ" is certainly optional.

Position some glasses to sit on display books or even on a plant. Add a pair or two on a simple, colorful banner that says:

or,

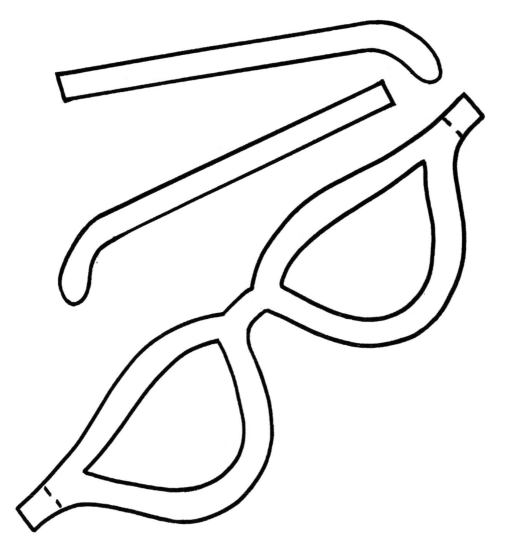

Keys

Create some giant key shapes from posterboard or large sheets of cardboard. Hang these from the ceiling or position them on the wall. These would be terrific ways to point out specific areas of the library including the checkout desk.

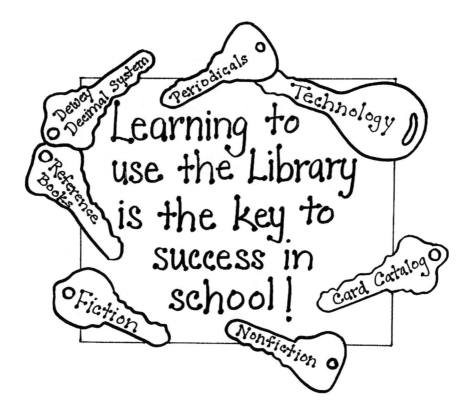

Friends

To make the paper dolls, fold a long strip of paper accordion style the width you would like your individual paper doll to be. Make some boy strips and an equal number of girl strips. Cut while the paper is folded. When the paper is opened to reveal the paper dolls, add a small construction paper book where the hands connect. This will help to honor the "friends tell friends" idea. Make several of these doll strips and staple the sections together.

To make some really large paper dolls, use a very long strip of poster paper. Fold it in the same manner and just enlarge your pattern. The size alone will be very attention-getting. Some giant paper dolls could be bent in half and set up against a backdrop as though they were sitting and books could be placed in their laps.

Have your students design a book cover for you for their favorite book. Your faculty might like to join in also, so be sure to extend the invitation. Provide them with the paper so that the covers will all be a uniform size. Talk to them about using a lot of color to create an appealing book cover and about writing legibly. Encourage them to print their message on the computer if that is a possibility.

Create a chain of the finished book covers to drape across the windows, around the door, and throughout the library. Use them also as a border for your bulletin board. Use all that are submitted so as not to hurt anyone's feelings.

Check your card catalog for books about friends and friendship. Arrange these with paper dolls draped among the books. The whole emphasis is on friends and books and how wonderful they both are to our lives.

Check your reference section for a book on quotations. Look up "friendship" to find some short quotes you could post around the room. During story time, try to read books that correlate with this theme. Also include books about ways to mend a broken friendship and how hard it is sometimes to stay friends. *Enemy Pie* is a great book to read.

Students may ask you to share some of your favorite books with them. Ahead of time, pull some of these to be ready to share.

Elephants

Elephants are popular characters in children's books. Us them as the focus of a bulletin board or display.

Create a head and ears for your elephant from gray construction paper. The head needs to be an oval that is a little wider at the top than at the bottom. Cut the two ears at the same time by using two 12" × 18" sheets of paper. The ears need to look large for the head.

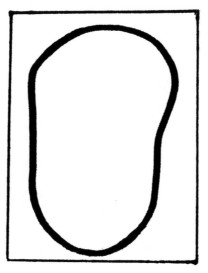

The trunk is made from a piece of dryer hose. One hose can be cut and used for more than one elephant. This hose comes in white or in a silver color, which looks great on an elephant. Position the hose by pinning it to the bulletin board. Add two eyes and you have a great elephant.

Use a construction paper book, a book cover, or a magazine cover positioned on the end of the elephant's trunk as though he's reading. Add any words you would like.

If you are a little more ambitious, make a whole elephant to fit a large wall space. This would work well cut out of a large piece of cardboard. If you use the dryer hose for the trunk, you may need to use a bolt and washer to hold it in place. A cardboard trunk would work fine, too.

Consider a phrase such as "You never forget a good book!"

Your elephant could be used with a zoo or circus display. For the circus, just add a colorful blanket on the elephant's back and a plume headdress.

The idea of using the dryer hose for the elephant's trunk also works terrifically for a game board for young children. Use a heavy piece of cardboard for the background. Paint the elephant's head or use gray construction paper as previously described. Attach the dryer hose with a bolt and washer.

Use candy peanuts for the game pieces. The children attempt to toss the candy peanut into the top of the dryer hose trunk. They really enjoy watching the candy pop out at the bottom of the trunk.

Before You Play the Game...

Use real balls with the Dewey Decimal number for that particular game attached. If you don't want to use real balls, create a paper basketball, baseball, etc. This could sit on top of the bookshelf in the 700s area of the library.

Basketball—796.323   Football—796.332
Baseball—796.357   Soccer—796.334

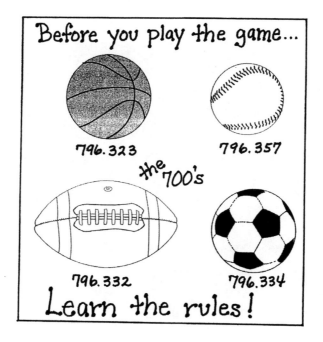

Before you play the game...

796.323   796.357

the 700's

796.332   796.334

Learn the rules!

Seeing Stars?

Place silver stars of all sizes on a black or dark blue background. Use a string of white lights (twinkling is really great if you can stand the distraction) for the border. On four stars write one letter each to spell out "READ" and place these stars in the center. Add a small note in the corner with directions: "Seeing stars? Check out the astronomy books in the 520s."

To make the display more 3-D, add stars hanging on fishing line. Vary the height of these stars.

Out of This World!

Create some reading aliens for this humorous display. Use a black background with some shiny silver stars and another planet in the distance. Make up some silly aliens. These are based on a silly song called "Vacuum Cleaner Hoses." In the song they are purple with neon green hair, three eyes,

and a vacuum cleaner nose. Make the alien out of construction paper. For hair, use strips of green paper folded or curled to stick out from the head. Glue on some roll-around-eyes, and use half of a plastic slinky for the nose.

Another suggestion for the background would be to just use a printed map of the solar system. Add some letters in a contrasting color to make them pop out.

Feature some of your science fiction collection. Be sure to include some from all different levels of difficulty.

Just to add a little more humor, print up some jokes or riddles about aliens and position them in the midst of the display. These bad jokes came from:

Jokelopedia: The Biggest, Best, Silliest, Dumbest Joke Book Ever [Compiled by Ilana Weitzman, New York: Workman Publishing Co., 2006.]

How can you tell if your dad's an alien?
   He knows how to program the VCR!

What did the alien say to the tree?
   Take me to your cedar.

Why did the earthling fall in love with the alien?
   Because she was out of this world!

Reading ... It's Like Magic!

Create an attention-getting tabletop display by making a top hat from a gallon can. (Ask the cooks in the cafeteria to save you a can.) Trace around the can onto a sheet of large black construction paper. Add four inches to the circle and that will become the brim for the top hat. Cut this out and slip it onto the can. Tape the brim in place. Use a sheet of black construction paper to cover the rest of the can and to cover the tape.

Use a toy stuffed rabbit placed in the hat posed to read a paper book. Use a piece of a dowel rod painted black with a silver end for a magic wand. Hang some sparkly stars around the hat. Add a sign to sit next to the hat with your message and add some books to finish up the display.

Library Snapshots

For a year long display that partially changes every week or so, consider creating a "Reading Star" display. Take digital photos of your students reading in the library or choosing their books. The pictures will be best if you are inconspicuous about taking them. Don't pose the children, be spontaneous.

Change these photos often to include as many children as possible in the display. This will keep them coming in to check the bulletin board to see if they are now "famous."

Use any background color that appeals to you, but using the school colors is always a plus. Include some gold or silver stars cut from poster board that are positioned among the photos.

If possible give the photos to the children when you take them off the bulletin board. For many children these will become prizes. Some children never get to experience being a star at anything.

No Need to Speed ...
Just Read and Enjoy!

Car racing is very popular these days. Create your own racecars by making construction paper books with wheels added. A black trash bag can be cut open and cut to size for a race track. The shine is great and it can just be tossed out when you are done with the display.

Either make some racing flags out of construction paper, or oftentimes, you can find black and white checkered paper sold as gift wrap or even as plastic tablecloths. Hang the flags around the room.

All kinds of slogans work well: "Ready ... Set ... Read!" "We're racing to read" or "Take one of our books for a test read."

Racing to Read!

Tired of Jumping Through Hoops?

This is a display idea for older students. It's difficult to learn to manage everything. This would be a good opportunity to get out those books on study skills or time management, and stress relieving books such as the *Chicken Soup for the Soul* books. Include a few joke books, too. We all need to laugh so much more!

Use hula hoops hung at various heights on fishing line. Hang a colorful sign in each hoop with some areas of student life listed. Add the words you feel are the most appropriate for this 3-D display.

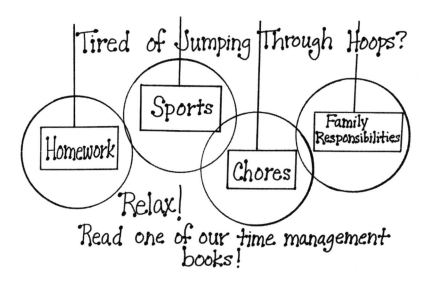

184

Conclusion

Hopefully at least one of these ideas appealed to you. The fact that you have looked through them is evidence that you are interested in additional ideas for marketing your library. Thank you for caring enough about your patrons to want to encourage them to read more.

Every library is different and the suggested ideas will need to be personalized for your particular library. Only you can make the right display for your setting. Have fun creating displays and let your personality and love of books shine through. An old saying applies: "No good deed goes unrewarded."

Index

Index